# A
# STUDENT'S
# DICTIONARY

## FOR BIBLICAL AND
## THEOLOGICAL STUDIES

# A STUDENT'S DICTIONARY

## FOR BIBLICAL AND THEOLOGICAL STUDIES

*F. B. HUEY, JR. and BRUCE CORLEY*

Academie Books from Zondervan Publishing House

1415 Lake Drive, S.E., Grand Rapids, Michigan 49506

A STUDENT'S DICTIONARY FOR BIBLICAL AND THEOLOGICAL STUDIES
Copyright © 1983 by The Zondervan Corporation
Grand Rapids, Michigan

**Library of Congress Cataloging in Publication Data**

Huey, F. B., 1925–
    A student's dictionary for biblical and theological
studies.

        Bibliography: p.
        1. Theology—Dictionaries.   2. Bible—Dictionaries.
I. Corley, Bruce C., 1943–   . II. Title.
BR95.H83   1983      220.6'03'21      83-16701
ISBN 0-310-45951-6

Designed by Louise Bauer
Edited by Ed M. van der Maas

ACADEMIE BOOKS are printed by Zondervan
Publishing House, 1415 Lake Drive, S.E.,
Grand Rapids, Michigan 49506

*Printed in the United States of America*

84  85  86  87  88  89 / 10  9  8  7  6  5  4  3  2

# Preface

A dictionary, by one of its definitions, is an alphabetically arranged collection of terms important for a field of study, defined in simple fashion. The business of making such a list has been ours for the past few years. We would seem to fall under Samuel Johnson's definition, typically pointed and humorous, of a lexicographer: "A harmless drudge, that busies himself in tracing the original, and detailing the signification of words" (*A Dictionary of the English Language*, 1775). Drudge indeed: for who can cover a subject that has no end and that requires little creativity save patience and a good filing system? For sanity's sake the following guidelines prevailed in the production of this dictionary.

The need for a specialized dictionary arises for the student who first encounters the overwhelming number of technical terms in biblical studies. The obvious gaps in dictionary help have been in the areas of language, grammar, and criticism. We have concentrated our effort here with, inevitably, some overlapping into wider theological jargon. The terms have been chosen with the theological student in mind who tackles the Hebrew and Greek texts along with their allied disciplines.

Our procedure was to make entries, over fourteen hundred, for those words occurring in grammars, commentaries, and similar reference works. We did not systematically include terms that would be more appropriate in a biblical or theological dictionary. The definitions are selective, brief, and simplified; the goal is to inform, not exhaust.

For wide-ranging terms it was tempting to become encyclopedic, but we tried (and perhaps failed) to heed the censure of pedantic definition, what A. T. Robertson called "the hundred and one distinctions in verbal anatomy . . . the rattle of dry bones" (*A Grammar of the Greek New Testament in the Light of Historical Research*, p. 1206). We assumed there to be more than one student who would have welcomed more definitions, at least grammatical ones, in reading Robertson's "big grammar."

Wherever possible, cross reference is made to related or equivalent terms, indicated by an arrow (→). A primary definition will be found at the reference word, e.g., the entries *complexive, global,* and *summary* are synonymous descriptions of a use of the Greek aorist tense defined under the entry →*effective aorist.*

In a majority of cases an entry is accompanied by examples from the Bible. Words in a biblical quotation that illustrate the term are printed in italics. Recourse to Hebrew and Greek will clarify the examples; these are introduced by the abbreviations *Heb:* and *Gk:,* meaning an example from the Hebrew Old Testament and the Greek New Testament respectively. Illustrations applicable to both languages or of a general nature are introduced by *Ex:* (example).

When an entry title contains more than one word or term, synonyms and alternate spellings are separated by a comma (STICH, STICHOS), different parts of speech, such as a noun and an adjective, by a slash (MESSIAH/MESSIANIC).

All of the biblical quotations (unless noted otherwise) are taken from the *New International Version* of the Bible published by Zondervan. Transliteration of Hebrew and Greek follows the scheme printed below, except for the conventional spelling of a few terms. For further reference we have appended a list of books that will be helpful to the student whose interest has been perked by this dictionary.

# Abbreviations for Books of the Bible

## OLD TESTAMENT

| | | | |
|---|---|---|---|
| Gen. | 1 Kings | Eccl. | Obad. |
| Exod. | 2 Kings | S. of Sol. | Jonah |
| Lev. | 1 Chron. | Isa. | Mic. |
| Num. | 2 Chron. | Jer. | Nah. |
| Deut. | Ezra | Lam. | Hab. |
| Josh. | Neh. | Ezek. | Zeph. |
| Judg. | Esth. | Dan. | Hag. |
| Ruth | Job | Hos. | Zech. |
| 1 Sam. | Ps. (Pss.) | Joel | Mal. |
| 2 Sam. | Prov. | Amos | |

## NEW TESTAMENT

| | | |
|---|---|---|
| Matt. | Eph. | Heb. |
| Mark | Phil. | James |
| Luke | Col. | 1 Peter |
| John | 1 Thess. | 2 Peter |
| Acts | 2 Thess. | 1 John |
| Rom. | 1 Tim. | 2 John |
| 1 Cor. | 2 Tim. | 3 John |
| 2 Cor. | Titus | Jude |
| Gal. | Philem. | Rev. |

# Hebrew Transliteration

| NAME | CONSONANT | TRANSLITERATION |
|------|-----------|-----------------|
| aleph | א | ʼ |
| beth | ב/בּ | b/b̠ |
| gimel | ג/גּ | g/g̠ |
| daleth | ד/דּ | d/d̠ |
| he | ה | h |
| waw | ו | w |
| zayin | ז | z |
| heth | ח | ḥ |
| teth | ט | ṭ |
| yod | י | y |
| kaph | ך ,כ/כּ | k/k̠ |
| lamed | ל | l |
| mem | ם ,מ | m |
| nun | ן ,נ | n |
| samek | ס | s |
| ayin | ע | ʻ |
| pe | פ/פּ | p/p̠ |
| sade | ץ ,צ | ṣ |
| qoph | ק | q |
| resh | ר | r |
| shin | שׁ | š |
| sin | שׂ | ś |
| taw | ת | t/t̠ |
| qames | ◌ָ | ā |
| pathah | ◌ַ | a |
| qames-he | (ה)◌ָ | â (h) |
| sere | ◌ֵ | ē |
| seghol | ◌ֶ | e |
| sere-yod | ◌ֵי | ê |
| hireq | ◌ִ | i |
| hireq-gadol | ◌ִי | î |
| holem | ◌ֹ | ō |
| qames-hatuph | ◌ָ | o |
| holem-male | וֹ | ô |
| qibbus | ◌ֻ | u |
| sureq | וּ | û |
| shewa | ◌ְ | e |
| hateph-pathah | ◌ֲ | a |
| hateph-seghol | ◌ֱ | e |
| hateph-qames | ◌ֳ | o |

# Greek Transliteration

| NAME | CAPITAL | SMALL | TRANSLITERATION |
|---|---|---|---|
| alpha | Α | α | a |
| beta | Β | β | b |
| gamma | Γ | γ | g |
| delta | Δ | δ | d |
| epsilon | Ε | ε | e |
| zeta | Ζ | ζ | z |
| eta | Η | η | ē |
| theta | Θ | θ | th |
| iota | Ι | ι | i |
| kappa | Κ | κ | k |
| lambda | Λ | λ | l |
| mu | Μ | μ | m |
| nu | Ν | ν | n |
| xi | Ξ | ξ | x |
| omicron | Ο | ο | o |
| pi | Π | π | p |
| rho | Ρ | ρ | r |
| sigma | Σ | σ,s | s |
| tau | Τ | τ | t |
| upsilon | Υ | υ | y |
| phi | Φ | φ | ph |
| chi | Χ | χ | ch |
| psi | Ψ | ψ | ps |
| omega | Ω | ω | ō |

## DIPHTHONGS

αι -- ai     οι -- oi

αυ --au     ου --ou

ει -- ei     υι -- ui

ευ --eu     ᾳ -- ā

ηυ --ēu     ῃ -- ē

               ῳ -- ō

## CLUSTERS

ῥ -- rh     γκ -nk

῾ -- h     γξ --nx

γγ ng     γχ --nch

**ABIOGENESIS.** An ancient belief that life can emerge from inanimate matter.

**ABLATIVE CASE.** This is the → case of separation in Greek; its form is the same as the → genitive, but its function is different. *Gk:* "They ran *out of the house* naked and bleeding" (Acts 19:16).

**ABLAUT.** The German term for → vowel gradation.

**AB OVO.** Latin for "from the egg." An expression used to mean "from the very beginning."

**ABSOLUTE.** In Hebrew Greek grammar, a word is absolute when it stands independently and has no grammatical relation to other elements in the sentence. The most common instance in Greek is the → genitive absolute.

**ABSOLUTE OBJECT.** Another name for → cognate accusative.

**ABSOLUTE STATE.** The Hebrew → absolute together with a word in the → construct state expresses the → genitive. Do not confuse with the → infinitive absolute. *Heb:* king (absolute); horse of (construct) the king (absolute), i.e., the king's horse (genitive). → Genitive Absolute.

**ABSTRACT NOUN.** → Noun.

**AB URBE CONDITA.** Latin for "from the founding of the city," abbreviated A.U.C. The Romans numbered their years from the founding of Rome. The date of this event, disputed among Roman historians, was established by Varro as 753 B.C. *Ex:* Herod the Great died in 750 A.U.C. = 4 B.C.

**ACCENT/ACCENTUATION.** In the biblical languages, a matter of stressed sound or force of utterance. Also a mark used in written Hebrew and Greek to indicate the nature and place of the spoken accent. See *Gesenius' Hebrew Grammar* (Kautzsch-Cowley 2nd ed.), section 15; and Robertson's *New Short Grammar of the Greek Testament*, sections 86–102.

**ACCIDENCE.** That part of grammar that treats → inflection; a subcategory of → morphology.

**ACCUSATIVE CASE.** A → substantive used as the direct object of a → transitive verb is said to be in the accusative → case. In Greek, the accusative is the case of extension. *Heb:* "In the beginning God created the *heavens* and the *earth*" (Gen. 1:1). *Gk:* "He gave the *right* to become children of God" (John 1:12).

**ACRONYM.** A word that is formed from the initial letters or groups of letters of the successive parts of a term of more than one word. *Ex:* BASOR = Bulletin of the American Schools of Oriental Research; *Ichthus* (Greek, "fish") = *Iēsous Christos Theou Uios Sotēr* (Jesus Christ, Son of God, Savior; the picture of a fish was a common sign among early Christians by which they identified themselves to one another). → Notarikon.

**ACROPHONY.** From Greek, "the sound of the initial [letter]." A term used to describe the manner in which letters of the alphabet originated. It is believed that the form of letters originally represented the rude outlines of concrete objects, the names of which began with the → consonant represented. Heb: *aleph*, derived from *eleph*, the old Hebrew word for ox; notice the two horns in the *aleph*.

**ACROSTIC.** In Hebrew poetry, an arrangement of successive words or phrases that begin with consecutive letters of the alphabet. There are a number of acrostics in the OT that are lost in translation. *Heb:* Pss. 111, 112, 119; Prov. 31:10–31; Lam. 1–4. There are no NT acrostics.

**ACTIVE VOICE.** In the active → voice, the → subject is the doer of the action that is expressed by the verb. *Heb:* "In the beginning *God created* the heavens and the earth" (Gen. 1:1). *Gk:* "*He gave* the right to become children of God" (John 1:12).

**ADD.** Abbreviation of Latin *addit* or *addunt*, "it adds" or "they add." Used in a → critical apparatus to refer to a reading added in a → manuscript.

**ADDAD.** A word that possesses mutually contradictory or contrasting meanings. *Heb:* ḥāḍal, "cease" or "continue"; *rāpā'*, "weaken" or "heal". *Gk: poieō*, "give" or "keep"; *erchomai*, "come" or "go."

**AD HOMINEM.** Latin, "to the man." An argument that is directed to one's prejudices rather than to one's intellect, or an argument that attacks the opponent rather than his arguments. *Gk:* the argument of Rom. 3:1–5 concludes, "I am using a human argument"; cf. Matt. 12:27. → Epidiorthosis.

**ADIAPHORA/ADIAPHORISTIC.** Greek for "things indifferent." A technical term in Stoic philosophy for things neither good nor evil. In Christian theology, matters not essential to faith, therefore neither required nor forbidden. *Ex:* the eating of meats sacrificed to idols (1 Cor. 8:4–13; 10:23–11:1).

**ADJECTIVE/ADJECTIVAL.** A word, → phrase, or → clause used to modify a → noun or in some cases a → substantive. In Hebrew and Greek, it agrees with the word modified (→ concord). *Heb:* "Abraham held a *great* feast" (Gen. 21:8). *Gk:* "I am the *good* shepherd" (John 10:11). Also called → *adnominal.*

**ADJUNCT.** A → modifier attached to the head of a → phrase, or a secondary element (such as an → adjective or → adverb), that can be removed without the structural identity of the construction being affected. *Ex:* "I went home *today*," or "I went home," but not "I went today."

**ADJUNCTIVE.** The use of a word, usually a → conjunction, to mean "also," "too." *Heb:* "She *also* gave some to her husband" (Gen. 3:6). *Gk:* "but *also* you can say to this mountain" (Matt. 21:21).

**AD LOC.** Abbreviation of Latin *ad locum,* "at the place." The place in a book referred to, the relevant passage to be consulted.

**ADNOMINAL.** A term used by some grammarians for → adjectival; a construction "related to the nominal" on analogy with → adverbial.

**ADONAI, ADONAY.** One of the names for God found in the OT; it is translated "Lord." *Heb:* "O Lord, I have never been eloquent" (Exod. 4:10). → Yahweh.

**ADOPTIONISM.** A → christological heresy of → Gnosticism, which holds that the human Jesus became divine or was possessed by the divine Christ at the time of His baptism; a form of → docetism ascribed to Cerinthus in Asia Minor at the end of the first century A.D.

**AD SENSUM.** A word or words written or translated according to meaning rather than precise grammatical → concord. *Ex:* a singular → collective noun may take a plural verb. *Heb:* "Let birds [sing.] fly above the earth" (Gen. 1:20); "My people [sing.] are destroyed [pl.] from lack of knowledge" (Hos. 4:6). *Gk:* "A very large crowd [sing.] spread [pl.] their cloaks" (Matt. 21:8).

**ADVERB/ADVERBIAL.** A word, → phrase, or → clause used to modify a verb, → adjective, or another adverb. In English, adverbs are usually formed with the → suffix -*ly*. In Hebrew and Greek, many adverbs are formed with suffixes; other parts of speech and many clauses are used adverbially. *Heb:* "Agag came to him *confidently*" (1 Sam. 15:32). *Gk:* "Freely you have received, *freely* give" (Matt. 10:8).

**ADVERBIAL CLAUSE.** A → subordinate clause that modifies the → main clause by defining the time, circumstance, purpose, cause, etc. of the action of the main verb. Major types are → temporal, → purpose, → result, → conditional, → causal, and → concessive.

**ADVERSATIVE.** The antithesis or contrary idea of a preceding word or → clause expressed by means of adversative → conjunctions, words, or clauses. *Heb:* "Your name will no longer be Jacob, *but* Israel" (Gen. 32:28). *Gk:* "Do not leave Jerusalem, *but* wait for the gift" (Acts 1:4).

**AETIOLOGY.** → Etiology.

**AFFIX.** A bound → morpheme, a letter or syllable placed at the beginning, middle, or end of a → root or → stem that will modify its meaning. *Heb:* → pronouns, plural endings, and verbal forms that indicate → person, → gender, and → number may be affixed to words. *Gk:* → *derivational* affixes are used to form new words, e.g., compounds like *kataphileō*, "I kiss," from *phileō;* → *inflectional* affixes include noun and verb endings, → augment, and → reduplication. → Infix, → Prefix, → Suffix.

**AFFORMATIVE.** An ending or → suffix.

**A FORTIORI.** Latin for "from the stronger (reason or argument)." The conclusion drawn is inferred to be even more certain than the preceding. → A Minore ad Majus, → Qal Waḥomer.

**AGAPE.** A → transliteration of one of the Greek words for "love" found in the NT. It is self-giving, self-sacrificing love, as contrasted to two other Greek words for "love," *eros* (fleshly, passionate love) and *philia* (brotherly love).

**AGGADAH.** → Haggadah.

**AGGLUTINATION/AGGLUTINATIVE.** From Latin, "to glue to." The running together or combining of words into → compound words in which the meaning and form of the separate parts undergo little or no change. *Ex:* English "afternoon." *Heb: ṣalmāweṭ,* "shadow of death" (Ps. 23:4). *Gk: archangelos,* "archangel."

**AGRAPHA.** Greek for "unwritten [sayings]." The sayings attributed to Jesus that are not found in the four Gospels but have some claim to be genuine. Also called *unknown* or *lost sayings. Ex:* the sayings scattered in the → Oxyrhynchus papyri or in the utterances of Paul (e.g., Acts 20:35; 2 Cor. 12:9).

**AGREEMENT.** → Concord.

**AKEDAH.** From Hebrew, "to bind." Name given to the offering of Isaac as a sacrifice by Abraham in Gen. 22:9. In Jewish thought, the supreme example of self-sacrifice in obedience to God's will and the symbol of Jewish martyrdom throughout the ages.

**AKHMIMIC.** A → Coptic dialect that was spoken in Upper Egypt. Extant Akhmimic texts date from the third to the fifth centuries A.D.

**AKKADIAN.** An early Semitic language that was written in → cuneiform. It became the major international language of the ancient Near East until replaced by → Aramaic in the first millennium B.C. The two most important dialects of Akkadian were Assyrian and Babylonian.

**AKTIONSART.** German for "kind of action." Used in grammars as the equivalent of → aspect.

**AL.** Abbreviation of Latin *alii*, "others." Used in a → critical apparatus to mean "other manuscripts read. . . ."

**ALALAKH TEXTS.** → Akkadian texts, dated between the seventeenth and fifteenth centuries B.C., that give information about the daily life, literature, and religion of Alalakh, a city near Antioch.

**ALEPH PROSTHETICUM.** Another name for → prosthetic *aleph*.

**ALEPPO CODEX.** A Hebrew → manuscript of the OT from the tenth century A.D., claimed to have been pointed (→ pointing) by Aaron ben Asher, the most illustrious member of the → Ben Asher family. Preserved, although with loss of a quarter of its → folios, and adopted for a new critical edition of the OT by the Hebrew University.

**ALEXANDRIAN TEXT.** A NT → text-type associated with Alexandria, Egypt; allegedly revised in the fourth century A.D. by the Egyptian bishop Hesychius. Its early form (called the neutral text by Westcott and Hort) includes the major witnesses Codex Sinaiticus and Codex Vaticanus. Also called *Egyptian*, *Hesychian*, or *Beta* text.

**ALIQ.** Abbreviation of Latin *aliqui*, "some." Used in a → critical apparatus to mean "some manuscripts read. . . ."

**ALLEGORY.** An interpretation that assumes that a text has a secondary and hidden meaning underlying its primary and obvious meaning; a story that presents its true meaning through figures; it has been called a prolonged → metaphor. Allegorical interpretation of the Bible was widespread in the early church. *Ex:* interpreted allegorically, the Song of Solomon deals with the love of Christ for His church; cf. Gal 4:24. → Typology.

**ALLITERATION.** Words or syllables that begin with the same sound. Alliteration is usually not retained when words are translated from one language to another. *Heb:* Ps. 122:6; Amos 5:5; Isa. 1:18–20. *Gk:* Rom. 1:29–30; 1 Peter 1:4.

**ALLOGRAPHY.** The use of a foreign → ideogram or → logogram in place of words from one's own language.

**ALLOMORPH.** A nonsignificant variant of a → morpheme, i.e., one of two or more forms that function identically. *Heb:* -ô and -hû are alternate forms of the third → person, singular noun → suffix. *Gk:* -as, -ous, and -a are alternate forms of the → accusative plural noun suffix. → Allophone.

**ALLOPHONE.** A nonsignificant variant of a → phoneme, i.e., one of two or more sounds that function identically. *Heb: w* and *v: w^esûs* and *v^esûs* both mean "and a horse." *Gk: o* and *ō: poma* and *pōma* both mean "drink." → Allomorph.

**ALLUSION.** In biblical studies, an implied or indirect reference to the OT in the NT by means of a common theme, word, or idea; a brief verbatim phrase that comes from the writer's vocabulary of faith, rather than an → explicit quotation of the OT text.

**ALPHA PRIVATIVE.** → Privative.

**ALPHA TEXT.** Another name for the → Byzantine text, or the → Lucianic text.

**ALTERNATIVE READING.** → Doublet, → Conflation.

**AMANUENSIS.** A → scribe or secretary hired to write from dictation; Paul frequently used an amanuensis (cf. Rom. 16:22; Gal. 6:11; Col. 4:18).

**AMBIGUOUS.** A word or phrase that may have more than one meaning in a specific context. *Heb:* "Ahab served Baal a little; Jehu will serve him much" (2 Kings 10:18). *Gk:* "Destroy this temple, and I will raise it again in three days" (John 2:19).

**AM HA'ARETS.** Hebrew for "people of the land." In the OT, the term is used variously to refer to all the people, the common people, or landowners; after the exile, to those Jews who had remained in the region around Jerusalem; in rabbinic literature, to a socio-religious class, viz., the common people who did not adhere to pharisaic regulations of purity, tithe, etc., in contrast to the → *haber.* Finally the term acquired the connotation "ignorant"; perhaps equivalent to the term "sinner" in the Gospels. *Heb:* "Be strong, all you people of the land" (Hag. 2:4). *Gk:* "I have not come to call the righteous, but sinners" (Matt. 9:13).

**AMIDAH.** → Eighteen Benedictions.

**A MINORE AD MAJUS.** Latin, "from the lesser to the greater." An argument that assumes "if such be true, then much more so the following." Equivalent to the rabbinic → *qal waḥomer* and hardly distinct from an argument → a fortiori. *Ex:* "Since we have now been justified by his blood, *how much more* shall we be saved from God's wrath through him!" (Rom. 5:9).

**AMMONIAN SECTIONS.** Divisions indicated in the margins of most Greek and Latin → manuscripts of the four Gospels; formerly thought to be the work of Ammonius Saccas, the → Neoplatonist philosopher, but probably devised by Eusebius, who numbered consecutively the sections in each Gospel and used them for cross reference in the → Eusebian canons.

**AMORAIM.** Hebrew, "speaker," "expounder." The collective name given to rabbis in Palestine and especially Babylon during the third through sixth centuries A.D., the successors of the → Tannaim. The Amoraim taught in the period after the → Mishnah and produced the → commentary on it called the → Gemara. → Zugoth.

**AMPHICTYONY.** Greek for "dwellers around." Denotes an association of tribes, cities, or other groups, such as the Delphic League or the Etruscan League, bound in common commitment to a deity and to the protection and service of his shrine. Martin Noth popularized this term in OT studies by his comparison of Israel's tribal organization to an amphictyony when it settled in Canaan; in recent years this comparison has been rejected by OT scholars.

**ANACHRONISM.** An error in chronology by which events, circumstances, or customs are misplaced in time, generally too early. *Ex:* when Shakespeare refers to the striking of a clock in *Julius Caesar,* he introduces an anachronism. *Heb:* the reference to the Philistines in Gen. 21:32 has frequently been called an anachronism, as it is believed that these people did not settle the eastern Mediterranean coast until ca. 1200 B.C.

**ANACOLUTHON.** Abandonment in the middle of a sentence of one type of construction in favor of a grammatically different one. *Heb:* Gen. 30:13; 31:32; Ezek. 34:10. *Gk:* Rom. 5:12–13; Gal. 2:4–6; Rev. 3:12.

**ANACRUSIS.** One or two unstressed syllables prefixed to a verse properly beginning with an accented syllable; a word at the beginning of a → stich that falls outside the pattern. *Ex:* "Therefore, . . ."

**ANADIPLOSIS.** Reduplication in poetry, where the second line of a couplet begins with the last or most prominent word of the first line. *Heb:* "*Ascribe* to the LORD, O mighty ones, *ascribe* to the LORD glory and strength" (Ps. 29:1).

**ANAGOGY/ANAGOGIC.** The spiritual meaning of a passage of Scripture as it relates to eternal or future realities.

*Ex:* Jerusalem is a type of the heavenly Jerusalem (Gal. 4:26). → Allegory, → Type.

**ANAGRAM.** A word or → phrase with meaning, formed by transposing the letters of another word or phrase. *Ex:* "Florence Nightingale" becomes "Flit on, cheering angel."

**ANALOGUE.** That which corresponds to something else; in biblical studies, specifically an earthly → analogy for something divine. *Ex: shepherd, father, king.*

**ANALOGY.** A comparison between two otherwise dissimilar things so that the one that is less known or understood is clarified by the other. *Gk:* Paul, who is fond of analogy, compares the love of a husband for his wife to that of Christ for the church (Eph. 5:25); 1 Cor. 14:6–8; 2 Tim. 2.3–7.

**ANALYTICAL LEXICON.** An alphabetically arranged list of all the major → parts of speech, including → nouns and → verbs in their → inflected forms, → parsed and defined. Analytical lexicons are available for the Hebrew and Aramaic OT and for the Greek NT. Also called a *parsing guide.*

**ANAPAESTIC RHYTHM, ANAPESTIC RHYTHM.** An ascending rhythm; the accented syllable stands at the end (see Otto Eissfeldt, *The Old Testament: An Introduction,* pp. 61–63).

**ANAPHORA.** The use of a word as a grammatical substitute for a preceding word or group of words ("I know *it* and he *does* too"); the repetition of a word or words at the beginning of successive clauses for emphasis or effect; also known as *epanadiplosis* and *epanaphora. Heb:* Ps. 150:1–5. *Gk:* Matt. 5:3–10; Acts 19:34; Heb. 11 ("by faith"). → Epiphora.

**ANAPHORIC ARTICLE.** The use of the definite article to refer back to a corresponding indefinite word in the preceding context. *Heb:* "*a* choice, tender calf . . . *the* calf that had been prepared" (Gen. 18:7–8); *Gk:* "given you living water . . . get *this* [lit., *the*] living water" (John 4:10–11).

**ANAPTYCTIC VOWEL.** From Greek, "to unfold." A term used to describe the development of a vowel from one form to another.

**ANAPTYXIS.** The insertion of a helping vowel. It usually occurs when two different consonants would close a syllable without the vowel. *Ex:* Some people pronounce *elm* as *el^em*. *Heb: tāwek̲* (the helping vowel is the *seghol*).

**ANARTHROUS.** A word that appears without the article is anarthrous. *Heb:* "Let us make *man*" (Gen. 1:26). *Gk:* "and the word was *God*" (John 1:1). → Articular.

**ANASTROPHE.** A change in the usual word order to emphasize a play on words; inversion of words or phrases in a sentence. *Heb:* "Noah walked with God" (Gen. 6:9); the word order is "with-God-walked-Noah." *Gk:* "Whoever sows sparingly will also reap sparingly" (2 Cor. 9:6); the word order is "whoever sows sparingly, sparingly . . ."

**ANATHEMA.** Greek for "accursed." A thing devoted to divine curse or eternal destruction; the NT usage is related to the OT concept of → *ḥerem*. Also called → *execration*. *Heb:* "anyone who is hung on a tree is under God's *curse*" (Deut. 21:23). *Gk:* "If anybody is preaching to you a gospel other than what you accepted, let him be *eternally condemned*" (Gal. 1:9).

**ANE.** Abbreviation used for the "ancient Near East."

**ANNEXION.** Another name for the construct-absolute relationship of nouns in the Hebrew language. The annexed word is the → construct, that to which annexion is made is the → absolute. *Heb:* "God set them in the expanse of [annexed/construct] the sky [absolute]" (Gen. 1:17).

**ANNOMINATIO.** A play on words where the sense and sound are alike. *Heb:* "a day of trouble [*šô'āh*] and ruin [*mᵉšô'āh*]" (Zeph. 1:15). *Gk:* "Do you understand [*ginōskeis*] what you are reading [*anaginōskeis*]?" (Acts 8:30). → Metaphone, → Paronomasia, → Parasonancy, → Parathesis.

**ANOMALY.** In grammar, an anomalous form is one that deviates from the general rule or is inconsistent with what would have been expected. *Heb:* in Gen. 1:18 the Hebrew word "and to separate" has a composite *shewa* under the *lamed* instead of the normal simple *shewa*. *Gk:* in 1 Thess. 2:8 the Greek word "we were delighted" retains an unaugmented → diphthong (→ augment) although the form is → imperfect.

**ANTANACLASIS.** The repetition of the same word with a different or even contrary meaning. *Heb:* "*comfort* them . . . *avenge* them" (Eccl. 4:1 NEB). *Gk:* "God made him who had no *sin* to be a *sin offering* for us" (2 Cor. 5:21 NIV mg).

**ANTECEDENT.** A → substantive to which a → pronoun refers; personal, demonstrative, and relative pronouns have antecedents. *Heb:* "a *nation whose* language you will not understand" (Deut. 28:49). *Gk:* "his *Son* from heaven, *whom* he raised from the dead" (1 Thess. 1:10).

**ANTEDILUVIAN.** Refers to the period of time before the Flood.

**ANTEPENULT, ANTEPENULTIMA.** In Greek, the third from the last syllable of a word. → Proparoxytone.

**ANTHROPOMORPHISM/ANTHROPOMORPHIC.** A description of God in human terms or with physical characteristics. *Ex:* "God saw" (Gen. 1:4), the "arm of the LORD" (Isa. 51:9), "the LORD smelled the pleasing odor" (Gen. 8:21). → Theomorphism.

**ANTHROPOPATHISM/ANTHROPOPATHY.** The attribution

of human emotions or feelings to God. *Heb:* "the Lord's anger" (Exod. 4:14), "You do not delight" (Ps. 51:16). *Gk:* "the kindness and sternness of God" (Rom. 11:22).

**ANTILEGOMENA.** Greek, "the ones spoken against." The books that were not accepted by all circles into the NT → canon or, more precisely, NT books that were disputed during the first three Christian centuries (see Eusebius, *Ecclesiastical History* 3.25). → Homologoumena.

**ANTINOMIANISM.** In biblical ethics, the attitude and practice of unlimited moral license, based on the assumption that grace means freedom to sin; a misunderstanding of Christian liberty. *Ex:* Rom. 3:8; 6:1–2; Gal. 5:13; 1 John 3:4–6. Also called *libertinism.*

**ANTIOCHENE TEXT.** Another name for the → Byzantine text.

**ANTIPHON/ANTIPHONAL.** A verse or verses spoken or sung responsively before and/or after a reading or song. *Ex:* Psalm 24 was probably sung antiphonally by pilgrims coming to Jerusalem.

**ANTIPHRASIS.** The use of a word when actually its opposite is intended. *Heb:* Job 2:9, where "bless" is in the Hebrew instead of the intended "curse." *Gk:* "You gladly put up with fools since you are so wise!" (2 Cor. 11:19). → Irony, → Litotes.

**ANTIPTOSIS.** An interchange of → cases that results in a confusion of grammatical relationships in a → phrase. *Gk:* "the consecrated bread" (Heb. 9:2), lit., "the presence of the bread," instead of "the bread of the presence" (cf. Matt. 12:4; Mark 2:26; Luke 6:4).

**ANTISTROPHE.** Another term for → epiphora.

**ANTITHESIS/ANTITHETICAL.** Contrast; a figure of speech in which words, → phrases, or → clauses (→ parallelism) are contrasted by being balanced one against the other. *Heb:* "For the LORD watches over *the way of the righteous,* but *the way of the wicked* will perish" (Ps. 1:6). *Gk:* "He was delivered over to *death* for our *sins* and was raised to *life* for our *justification*" (Rom. 4:25).

**ANTITHETIC PARALLELISM.** In Hebrew poetry, the second line of a couplet contrasts with the thought of the first by means of a contradictory or opposing statement, thereby intensifying the thought of the first line. *Ex:* Prov. 10:1.

**ANTONOMASIA.** A figure of speech in which a popular epithet, characteristic trait, or activity is substituted for a proper name. *Heb:* "the city of the Great King [= God]" (Ps. 48:2). *Gk:* "the disciple whom Jesus loved [= the apostle John]" (John 21:20). → Periphrasis, → Circumlocution.

**ANTONYM, ANTONYMY.** A word that is approximately opposite in meaning and use to another. *Ex:* "bad" is an antonym of "good." *Heb:* "God called the *light 'day'* and the *darkness* he called *'night'* " (Gen. 1:5).

**AORIST TENSE.** The Greek aorist → tense depicts the action of the verb from an undefined, summary viewpoint; it presents the action as → punctiliar, whatever the action actually is. In the → indicative mood it is the simple past tense, corresponding to the Hebrew → perfect. *Gk:* "death came to all men because all *sinned*" (Rom. 5:12). Emphases of the tense in historical narrative include → constative, → inceptive, and → effective.

**AP.** Abbreviation of Latin *apud,* "in" or "among." Used in → textual criticism as a general reference, "in the writings of. . . ."

**APHAERESIS, APHERESIS.** The dropping of a letter or syllable from the beginning of a word. *Heb: qaḥ* for *leqaḥ* (Jonah 4:3). *Gk: thelō* for *ethelō.* → Apocopation.

**APHORISM.** A short, pithy statement of a general truth; a maxim. *Heb:* Prov. 13:1; *Gk:* Gal. 6:7.

**APOCALYPSE/APOCALYPTIC.** Greek, "to uncover," "unveil." A disclosure of the future that is viewed as prophetic revelation. It concerns the overthrow of the present age and the establishment of God's rule. As a → genre, a group of OT, intertestamental, and NT texts featuring vision, symbol, and historical determinism. *Ex:* Daniel 7–12 (OT), Enoch (→ Pseudepigrapha), and Revelation (NT).

**APOCALYPSE, THE.** Another name for the book of Revelation.

**APOCALYPSE, THE LITTLE.** The prophecy of the destruction of Jerusalem in Mark 13; the term was introduced by T. Colani (1864), who viewed the discourse as a composite based on an interpolated Jewish-Christian → apocalypse.

**APOCOPATION.** To cut short by apocope, i.e., the rejection of a letter or syllable at the end of a word. *Heb:* The loss of the final *he* in many Hebrew words. *Gk:* The loss of a final short vowel before an initial consonant in Greek composition. → Aphaeresis.

**APOCRYPHA/APOCRYPHAL, OT.** A large group of Jewish writings outside the OT → canon that were composed between 200 B.C. and A.D. 200. They are included in the → Septuagint and the Latin → Vulgate.

**APOCRYPHA/APOCRYPHAL, NT.** A collective term for → noncanonical literature produced by the early church that develops forms present in the NT, viz., gospels, acts, epistles, and → apocalypses. For the most part, spurious writings that served the → Gnostic tendency and rivaled their NT counterparts.

**APOCRYPHON.** A term used to describe a → noncanonical, → pseudonymous writing of the → intertestamental or early church periods that qualifies for, but is not included in, the traditional collections of → Apocrypha and → Pseudepigrapha. *Ex:* the Genesis Apocryphon from Qumran.

**APODICTIC LAW.** A law that is stated in absolute terms; cf. → casuistic law. *Heb:* the OT laws introduced by "you shall" (Exod. 20:3–17).

**APODOSIS.** The conclusion in a → conditional sentence, expressing the result of a → protasis; the independent or "then" clause. *Heb:* "If you fully obey the LORD your God . . . [protasis], the LORD your God will set you high above all the nations on earth [apodosis]" (Deut. 28:1). *Gk:* "If you love me [protasis], you will obey what I command [apodosis]" (John 14:15).

**APOLLONIAN CANON.** A rule concerning the Greek article with nouns in → regimen (formulated by Apollonius Dyscolus, fl. second century A.D.), which asserts that a noun and its → genitive either both take the article (e.g., Col. 1:5) or neither (e.g., 2 Cor. 6:7). The rule is modified in NT usage.

**APOLOGIA.** Greek for "apology" or "defense." A reasoned verbal defense or explanation of one's conduct; also a rhetorical → genre in the → Second Sophistic. *Ex:* Christian apologies by Paul (Acts 26:1–29) and harassed believers (1 Peter 3:15).

**APOPHASIS.** A pretended suppression of what the writer or speaker really intends to say. *Heb:* Amos 4:4. *Gk:* Philem. 19. → Paralipsis

**APOPHTHEGM.** → Apothegm.

**APOSIOPESIS.** The concealment or suppression of an entire sentence or clause, which, because it is necessary to complete the sense, must be supposed from the context; a sudden break in the sentence. *Heb:* "If you don't" (1 Sam. 2:16) means "If you will not give it to me." *Gk:* Luke 19:42; Acts 23:9; 2 Cor. 3:13.

**A POSTERIORI.** Latin for "from the latter (effect)." Argument from inductive reasoning; derived by reasoning from observed facts or experience; the opposite of → a priori.

**APOSTOLIC AGE.** The earliest period of church history, co-extensive with the activity of the apostles; generally dated A.D. 30 to A.D. 100, from the founding of the Jerusalem church to the death of the apostle John.

**APOSTOLIC FATHERS.** Conventional title given to the Greek church fathers immediately following the → apostolic age; the collection of Greek → patristic writings that date from the early second century A.D.: the letters of Clement of Rome, Ignatius of Antioch, Polycarp, and Barnabas, the Shepherd of Hermas, the Didache, the fragments of Papias, and the letter to Diognetus.

**APOSTOLICON.** Greek for "that relating to an apostle." Used variously by the Greek church fathers to refer to an apostolic writing, a collection of epistles (Marcion's term for Paul's letters), or a → lectionary of one of the NT → epistles.

**APOSTROPHE.** A sign used in English and Greek to indicate the omission of one or more letters from a word (→ elision); the same sign is also used to indicate → smooth breathing and → coronis. Also, a figure of speech in which a person (usually absent) or personified thing is addressed rhetorically, as if present and capable of understanding. *Heb:* "Hear, O heavens! Listen, O earth!" (Isa. 1:2). *Gk:* "Now you, if you call yourself a Jew" (Rom. 2:17).

**APOTHEGM, APOPHTHEGM.** A short, pithy saying that expresses an important truth in a few words; a maxim. In → form criticism, a technical term for a saying of Jesus set in a brief narrative context. *Ex:* Mark 2:23–28. Also called → *paradigm.* → Pronouncement Story, → Chreia.

**APPARATUS CRITICUS.** Latin for → critical apparatus.

**APPELLATIVE.** A → common noun (as opposed to a → proper noun). Sometimes appellatives assume the complete character of true proper names. *Heb:* '*elōhîm*, a Hebrew word for "gods," can also mean "God." *Gk: kurios,* a Greek word for "lord," is also the name, "Lord [Jesus Christ]."

**APPOSITION/APPOSITIVE.** A word, → phrase, or → clause placed after a → substantive to rename or explain it. *Heb:* "A widow" (1 Kings 7:14), lit., "a woman, a widow." *Gk:* "him as a sacrifice" (Rom. 3:25); "James, a servant" (James 1:1). → Epexegetical, → Permutation.

**A PRIORI.** Latin for "from the former (cause)." Argument from deductive reasoning; derived by reasoning from self-evident presuppositions; the opposite of → a posteriori.

**AQUILA.** A Christian, ca. A.D. 130, who converted to Judaism and produced a Greek translation of the Hebrew Bible that had an extremely literalistic style. → Hexapla.

**ARAMAIC.** A branch of the northwest Semitic languages that is closely related to Hebrew. In the OT → Masoretic text, Ezra 4:8–6:18; 7:12–26; Dan. 2:4b–7:28; and Jer. 10:11 are in Aramaic rather than Hebrew. Aramaic had become the common language of the Jewish people by NT times. → Aramaism.

**ARAMAISM.** The insertion of an Aramaic word where a Hebrew or Greek word should have appeared, or a feature of NT language that reflects Aramaic influence. *Ex:* "Rabboni" (John 20:16). → Semitism.

**ARCHAISM.** The preservation (or insertion) of an earlier or more primitive word or expression.

**ARCHETYPE.** A → manuscript that is not the immediate parent of another but is a remoter ancestor.

**ARETALOGY.** A collection of miracle stories, a celebration of the deeds and/or vitures of a god, or a biography of a semidivine being or religious hero. *Ex:* Philostratus' *Life of Apollonius of Tyana.*

**ARGUMENTUM E SILENTIO.** Latin for "argument from silence." An interpretation based on the silence of the Scriptures, often on the assumption that because a biblical writer did not mention an event he was ignorant of it or it had not happened when he wrote. *Heb:* the scarcity of messages by Jeremiah during the reign of Josiah is used as an argument that he was not totally supportive of Josiah's reforms. *Gk:* the letters of Paul must have been collected after the writing of Acts since otherwise Luke would have referred to them.

**ARTICULAR.** A word that appears with the definite article is articular. *Heb:* "God saw that *the light* was good" (Gen. 1:4). *Gk:* "He himself was not *the light*" (John 1:8). → Anarthrous.

**ASCENSIVE.** The use of a word, usually a → conjunction, to increase the force or intensity of a statement; it may be argumentative or climactic. *Gk: kai* in *kagō,* "even I" (Rom. 3:7), forming an "ascent" to the *egō* by a tacit comparison, "why am I still condemned?"

**ASCETICISM.** A lifestyle designed to combat vice and develop virtue by self-denial and, in exaggerated forms, withdrawal from society.

**ASHERAH.** A sacred pole or tree that was used in the Canaanite fertility rites; also the goddess of the same name. → KJV translates the word as "groves."

**ASHKENAZIC.** A pronunciation of the Hebrew language that developed among the Ashkenazim, the Jews in middle and northern Europe, especially Germany, in contrast to → Sephardic.

**ASIANISM.** A tendency in → Hellenistic oratory and prose of the second century B.C. toward bombast and affected style; named after the highly ornamental Greek of Asia Minor. → Atticism.

**ASPECT.** A category used in grammatical analysis of the verb (along with → tense and → mood) to describe the duration or kind of action; the English equivalent of the German technical term → *Aktionsart. Heb:* the → perfect represents completed action, as opposed to the → imperfect, which represents incomplete action. *Gk:* the → present tense represents linear, progressive action, while the → aorist represents punctiliar action.

**ASPIRATE/ASPIRATION.** Sounded with a strong emission of breath; addition of an *h* sound to a → phoneme, especially to the vowel beginning a Greek word; indicated in writing by a rough → *breathing mark.* → Spirant.

**ASSEVERATIVE/ASSEVERATION.** A word or phrase that expresses the idea of certainty; an emphatic or earnest affirmation, particularly used in oaths (e.g., "As the Lord lives," "Far be it from me"). It may express simple asseveration (1 Sam. 2:30; 2 Sam. 20:20) or may introduce promises or threats confirmed by an oath. *Heb:* there are few examples of an asseverative *kî;* "[surely (*kî*)] your love is more delightful than wine" (Song of Sol. 1:2); "Surely [*'im lō'*, lit., "if not"] as I have planned" (Isa. 14:24). *Gk:* the → particles *ei mēn* introduce asseverative statements, e.g., "I will surely [*ei mēn*] bless you" (Heb. 6:14). More common forms include "Yes, I tell you" (Luke 12:5); "I speak the truth" (Rom. 9:1); "I am not lying" (2 Cor. 11:31); and oath-taking (e.g., Mark 5:7).

**ASSIMILATION.** The adaptation of two adjacent sounds (consonant or vowel) to each other, either forward (progressive assimilation) or backward (regressive assimilation) in the word. Generally, a consonant that should close a syllable passes over into another that begins the next syllable and forms with it a strengthened letter or syllable. *Heb: nun* is the most frequently assimilated letter in Hebrew, e.g., *yiqqātēl:* the → *daghesh forte* in

31

the *qoph* represents an assimilated *nun* of the → niphal stem. *Gk:* a consonant that precedes a consonant is generally assimilated to the second consonant, e.g., in *emmenō, n + m* has become *mm.*

**ASSONANCE.** Similarity of sound in the accented vowels. *Heb:* repetition of the *û* sound in Isa. 53:4–7, of the *ē* sound in Ezek. 27:27. *Gk:* repetition of the *ou* sound in Eph. 1:3. Some examples of assonance in the NT resemble the → Gorgian figures of classical rhetoric. → Paronomasia.

**ASV.** Abbreviation of *American Standard Version,* an American revision of the *Revised Version* (1881–1885) of the *King James Version* (1611); it was first published in 1901.

**ASYNDETON.** Omission of → conjunctions or → particles that would ordinarily join → coordinate words or sentences together. *Heb:* "Go, walk" (Gen. 13:17). *Gk:* "I tell you, get up, take your mat" (Mark 2:11).

**ATHBASH, ATBASH.** A coded language in which the first letter of the alphabet represents the last, the second letter the next to the last, etc. *Heb:* Sheshach = Babylon (Jer. 25:26).

**ATHEMATIC VERB.** → Thematic Verb.

**ATHETIZE.** The rejection of a passage or text on the grounds that it is spurious.

**ATHNAH.** → Pause.

**ATTENUATION.** The "thinning" of a sound. *Heb:* A *pathah* may become a *hireq,* or a full vowel may be reduced to a *shewa. Gk:* any of the long vowels may be shortened in formation and → inflection of words; cf. → vowel gradation.

**ATTICISM.** The archaist revival of the classical Greek dialect in the prose and oratory of the early Roman empire; a reaction to → Asianism. In writing, Atticisms derive from an admiration for or imitation of classical grammar and style. *Gk:* Attic → reduplication, which both reproduces the first syllable and lengthens the → stem vowel: *akouō* becomes *akēkoa*.

**ATTRIBUTIVE.** An → adjective or other → adjunct word that stands before the noun it qualifies. *Ex: white* bread. *Heb:* the attributive may also be expressed by the → genitive relationship: "man of strength" = "strong man." *Gk:* the attributive may follow the noun when both are → articular.

**A.U.C.** Abbreviation for → Ab Urbe Condita.

**AUGMENT.** In Greek, a → prefix denoting past time in the verb, added to the → imperfect, → aorist, and → pluperfect → tenses of the → indicative mood (→ secondary tenses). The prefix *e* added to verbs beginning with a consonant is called *syllabic augment;* the lengthening of the initial vowel of a verb beginning with a vowel is called *temporal augment.*

**AUTHORIZED VERSION.** → AV.

**AUTOCHTHONOUS.** That which is native or indigenous; the word has been used to describe tribes.

**AUTOGRAPH.** The original → manuscript in the author's own handwriting or dictated to an → amanuensis by the author. No autographs of biblical texts have been discovered. → Urrolle.

**AUTOSOTERISM.** The belief that a person can save himself by his own efforts.

**AUXILIARY VERB.** A "helping" verb, one that helps to form the compound tenses. *Ex:* "He *has* eaten," "they *will* go."

**AV.** Abbreviation for *Authorized Version,* another name for the *King James Version* of the Bible. → KJV.

**BABYLONIAN TALMUD.** → Gemara.

**BARAITA.** Aramaic for "external." Sayings of the → Tannaim not included in the → Mishnah. Preserved in various → midrashim, in the largest systematic collection called the → *Tosephta*, and scattered throughout the → Talmud.

**BARTH'S LAW.** A statement of predictable vowel changes in Hebrew. If the → thematic vowel of the → perfect is *a*, the thematic vowel of the → imperfect will be of the *u*-class. If the perfect thematic vowel is *i* or *u*, the imperfect will be *a*.

**BARYTONE.** In Greek, a word that has no accent on the last syllable, or → ultima. → Oxytone, → Paroxytone.

**BASE.** Another term for → stem.

**BATH QOL, BATH KOL.** Hebrew for "daughter of a voice." A rabbinic term for the heavenly voice that revealed God's will after the cessation of prophecy. The *bath qol* could give divine approval of → halakic rulings; some scholars apply this background to the interpretation of Jesus' baptism.

**B. C. E.** Abbreviation of "Before the Common Era" (sometimes understood as "Before the Christian Era"). It is used as a "neutral" substitute for B.C. ("Before Christ").

**BEGAD KEPHAT LETTERS.** A → mnemonic device containing six Hebrew consonants (*beth, gimel, daleth, kaph, pe, taw*) whose pronunciation may change by the insertion or omission of a → *daghesh lene.*

**BEING, VERB OF.** Another name for → copula.

**BEN.** Hebrew for "son." *Ex:* Benjamin means "son of the right hand."

**BEN ASHER TEXT.** The Hebrew OT text as vocalized by the Tiberian → Masoretes of the Ben Asher family, completed ca. A.D. 900. Sometimes called the → *textus receptus.* The normative form of the → Masoretic text, used in modern critical editions of the OT. → Cairo Prophets, → Aleppo Codex, → Leningrad Codex.

**BENEDICTIONS, PAULINE.** Stereotyped → formulas of → blessing used to conclude a letter, usually after a series of greetings and a doxology. *Gk:* 1 Thess. 5:28; 1 Cor. 16:23; Phil. 4:23. → Berakah.

**BENEDICTUS.** Name of Zechariah's hymn concerning John the Baptist (Luke 1:68–79), derived from the opening word of the Latin text: "*Benedictus Dominus,*" "Praise be to the Lord."

**BERAKAH (pl., BERAKOT).** Hebrew for "blessing," "benediction." A biblical → formula of praise and thanksgiving; rabbinic Judaism prescribed recitation of blessings in the prayer service and daily life. *Heb:* "Praise be to you, O Lord" (Ps. 119:12); this phrase occurs in every Jewish blessing. *Gk:* the liturgical form appears in NT epistolary literature; Eph. 1:3; 1 Peter 1:3. → Blessing.

**BERESHITH.** Hebrew name for the Book of Genesis ("In the beginning").

**BERITH.** Hebrew for "covenant."

**BETA TEXT.** Another name for the → Alexandrian text.

**BETH ESSENTIAE.** After ideas of appearing, manifesting oneself, representing, or being, *beth* is used in Hebrew in the sense of "as," "in the capacity of," "consisting of." *Heb:* "I appeared to Abraham, to Isaac and to Jacob *as* God Almighty" (Exod. 6:3).

**BH.** Abbreviation used to designate Kittel's *Biblica Hebraica;* third edition published 1937; sometimes abbreviated BH3, BHK.

**BHK.** → BH.

**BHS.** Abbreviation of *Biblia Hebraica Stuttgartensia,* a complete revision of → BH; published in its entirety in 1977.

**BH3.** → BH.

**BIBLICAL CRITICISM.** A term used loosely to describe all the methodologies applied to the study of the biblical texts.

**BIBLICISM/BIBLICIST.** Uncritical and extremely literal interpretation of the Scriptures.

**BIBLIOGRAPHY.** An alphabetically arranged list of books and articles that are pertinent to a given subject.

**BIBLIOLATRY.** Excessive reverence for the Bible that makes it into a sacred object, usurping the place of the God of the Bible who properly should be the object of reverence.

**BIBLIOPHILE.** One who loves books.

**BICOLA, BICOLON.** Two cola (→ colon).

**BIOS.** Greek for "life." The ancient literary term for a biography; some scholars argue that the Gospels are a type of *bios* literature.

**BIS.** Latin for "twice." Used in a → concordance or index to indicate the double occurrence of a word in a single verse.

**BISTICH.** Two stichs (→ stich). → Distich.

**BLESSING.** Words spoken or written to extol the praise of God and pronounce divine care upon the hearer; → performative utterances that bring happiness, wholeness, or praise. *Heb:* "The LORD bless you and keep you . . . and give you peace" (Num. 6:24–26). *Gk:* "To him who sits on the throne and to the Lamb be praise" (Rev. 5:13). → Berakah, → Benediction.

**BORROWING.** A term used to describe the use of a foreign word or words. → Loanword.

**BOUND FORM.** A type of → morpheme.

**BOUSTROPHEDON.** The practice of writing lines alternately from right to left and from left to right.

**BRACHYLOGY.** The omission of the common object of a verb or of a sentence element necessary to the thought but not to the structure. *Gk:* "*Tell me* so that I may believe on him" (John 9:36; "Tell me" is not in the Greek). → Ellipsis, → Pregnant Construction.

**BREATHING MARKS.** In Greek, every vowel or diphthong at the beginning of a word is marked with the sign of smooth breathing (') or rough breathing ('), also called *spiritus lenis* and *spiritus asper*. Rough breathing introduces → aspiration, the sound *h* preceding the pronunciation, whereas smooth breathing indicates its absence. *Gk: horos*, "boundary"; *oros*, "mountain."

**BRITISH LIBRARY CODEX.** A Hebrew manuscript of the → Pentateuch, probably from the tenth century A.D.; a →

Ben Asher text, whose name is frequently mentioned in the margins.

**"BUMP" LETTERS.** A → mnemonic device containing the Hebrew consonants that affect the pronunciation of the conjunction *waw* when it is prefixed to these consonants. The rule is that before *beth, mem, pe,* and *shewa* the conjunction is pointed *wû* instead of $w^e$ (→ pointing).

**BYZANTINE TEXT.** The NT → text-type associated with Byzantium and the Greek East, found in the majority of later → manuscripts and usually the majority → reading of a passage. Probably revised at Antioch of Syria in the fourth century A.D. (→ *Lucianic text*). It is the basis of the → textus receptus. Also called *Syrian, Koine, Alpha,* or *Antiochene text.*

**C.** Abbreviation of the Latin word *circa,* "about," "approximately." *Ex:* David became king c. 1020 B.C. Also abbreviated *ca.*

**CA.** → *C.*

**CAESURA.** A break in a verse, usually according to the sense and usually near the middle of the verse; a major stop or pause.

**CAIRO PROPHETS.** A Hebrew manuscript of the → Prophets, written by Moses → *ben Asher* ca. A.D. 895; the oldest extant → Masoretic text. It is owned by the Karaite community in Cairo. Also called *Codex Cairensis.*

**CALLIGRAPHER.** One who is skilled at beautiful or elegant handwriting.

**CANON.** The books of the Bible that have been accepted as inspired and authoritative. The OT is the Jewish canon, the OT and NT together form the Christian canon.

**CANONICAL.** Pertaining to the books or parts of the OT and NT that form the → canon.

**CANONICAL CRITICISM.** Study of the biblical texts as we now have them and as they have been transmitted through the centuries.

**CANTICLES, CANTICLE OF CANTICLES.** Another name for the Song of Songs; also called the *Song of Solomon.*

**CAPTATIO BENEVOLENTIAE.** Latin term for the rhetorical "capture of the good will" of one's hearer or reader by compliant or flattering speech; a conventional device at the beginning of an oration to win a favorable hearing. A feature of Paul's epistolary style. *Heb:* Jacob to Esau (Gen. 32:3–5). *Gk:* Paul to Agrippa (Acts 26:2–3; cf. 24; 2–4, 10).

**CARDINAL.** Short for cardinal number (one, two, three, etc.). → Ordinal.

**CASE.** Case shows the grammatical relation of → inflected forms such as → nouns and → pronouns to other words (nominative, possessive, objective cases).

**CASE ENDING.** In Greek, case endings are affixed to words to designate the → case; in Hebrew, case endings are no longer used except in rare instances that may be remnants of earlier case endings.

**CASE LAW.** → Casuistic Law.

**CASUISTIC LAW.** A law that is stated in conditional terms; the key word is "if"; sometimes called *case law. Heb:* "*If* a man has a stubborn and rebellious son" (Deut. 21:18–19). → Apodictic Law.

**CASUS INSTRUMENTALIS.** Latin for → instrumental case.

**CASUS PENDENS.** The logical subject is placed in an isolated position or form and its → predication follows in a distinct and sometimes recast sentence, → nominal or → verbal. In Greek, the commonly suspended case is the → nominative (called *nominative absolute*), though → oblique forms can also be isolated. *Heb:* "As for God, his way is perfect" (Ps. 18:30), lit., "God, his way is perfect." *Gk:* Rev. 3:21; Acts 7:40; John 1:33.

**CATECHESIS/CATECHETIC.** Oral instruction in one's faith or a collection of written materials used for this purpose. → Form criticism believes that catechetical needs were responsible for the formation of some of the Scriptures.

**CATENA.** A commentary (lit., "chains" of comments) that accompanies the biblical text in some → LXX → manuscripts. It was compiled from various sources, such as the church fathers, Josephus, Philo, etc. The word can also mean a series of quotations, sayings, miracle stories, etc. *Ex:* the chain of OT quotations in Rom. 9:25–29.

**CATHOLIC EPISTLES.** Title assigned by Eusebius (*Ecclesiastical History* 2.23) to seven NT letters; James, 1–2 Peter, 1–3 John, and Jude. The term *katholikē* (Greek, "universal") was apparently used in the sense "addressed to all the churches," although 2–3 John and 1 Peter have specific addressees. Also called *General Epistles.*

**CAUSAL CLAUSE.** A type of → adverbial clause that answers the question "because of what?"; introduced in English by *because. Heb:* "*Because* you did not trust . . . you will not bring" (Num. 20:12). *Gk:* "men loved darkness instead of light *because* their deeds were evil" (John 3:19).

**CAUSATIVE VERB.** A → transitive verb that can be said to cause the action depicted in a corresponding → intransitive verb. *Ex: lay* ("cause to lie") is the causative of *lie; raise,* the causative of *rise.*

**C.E.** Abbreviation of "Common Era" (sometimes understood as "Christian Era"). It is used as a "neutral" substitute for A.D. (Anno Domini, "in the year of [our] Lord").

**CENTO.** A literary composition that is formed from various selected sources; a patchwork. In biblical criticism the term refers to scriptural quotations. *Ex:* Matt. 11:10; Gal. 4:27; Heb. 8:8–12. → Catena, → Florilegium.

**CHANUKKAH.** → Hanukkah.

**CHARISMA/CHARISMATIC.** Greek for "gift," "a favor bestowed." A spiritual gift, an endowment of God's grace bestowed by the Holy Spirit. "Charismatic" refers to a person who claims spiritual gifts, or to behavior performed in the power of such gifts. *Gk:* "Now about spiritual gifts" (1 Cor. 12:1).

**CHESED.** Alternate transliteration of → ḥesed.

**CHIASMUS, CHIASTIC.** An arrangement of the parallel members of a verse or literary unit to form an a-b-b-a arrangement (the first line corresponds to the fourth, the second to the third). Chiasmus is also called inverted or introverted → parallelism; extended patterns appear in Hebrew and Greek. *Heb:* Ps. 30:8–10; Gen. 4:4b–5a. *Gk:* Rom. 10:9–10; 1 Cor. 1:24–25; Philem. 5.

**CHIASTIC PARALLELISM.** Another name for → inverted parallelism.

**CHILIASM/CHILIASTIC.** From the Greek word "thousand." The belief that Christ will return to reign on earth for a thousand years (Rev. 20). Synonymous with millennialism/ millennial.

**CHREIA.** A concise account of statements or deeds of a particular person that provides guidance for conduct; especially a brief narrative → pericope built around a striking saying of Jesus. *Ex:* the widow's mite (Luke 21:1–4). → Apothegm.

**CHRESTOMATHY.** A selection of passages compiled as an aid to learning a language. *Ex:* a student's reader in Hebrew or Greek.

**CHRISTOLOGY/CHRISTOLOGICAL.** That part of theological

study or affirmations relating to the person and work of Christ, especially the union in Him of the human and the divine.

**CIRCUMLOCUTION.** A roundabout way of expressing something that could be stated more directly or in fewer words. *Heb:* The Hebrew language does not have a verb "to have," so the idea must be expressed by circumlocution: "We have an aged father" (Gen. 44:20) is literally, "There is to us an aged father." *Gk:* It is commonplace in the verb and genitive constructions dependent on the → LXX. → Periphrasis, → Antonomasia.

**CIRCUMSTANTIAL CLAUSE.** The statement of the particular circumstances under which the action of the main clause takes place. *Heb:* "As the sun was setting, Abram fell into a deep sleep" (Gen. 15:12). *Gk:* The Greek → participle performs this function in a wide variety of ways: temporal, causal, conditional, etc. "When God raised up [temporal participle] his servant, he sent him" (Acts 3:26).

**CITATION.** → Explicit Quotation.

**CJ.** Abbreviation of Latin *coniectura*, "conjecture." In → textual criticism and in a → critical apparatus, the conjectural reading of a → manuscript. Also abbreviated *conj.*

**CLAUSE.** A clause may compose all or part of a complete sentence; it consists of a subject and predicate. In terms of function in the sentence, clauses are of three types: → main, → subordinate, and → coordinate.

**CLIMACTIC PARALLELISM.** In Hebrew poetry, part of the first line of a couplet is repeated and becomes the point of departure as the thought proceeds step by step to a climax; also called stairlike or repetitive parallelism. The pattern is described as a-b-c/a-b-d. *Ex:* Ps. 29:1–2.

**CLIMAX.** Greek, "ladder." A rhetorical figure in which a series of ideas is organized in ascending fashion to reach a crescendo. *Heb:* "he will heal . . . he will bind up . . . he will revive . . . he will restore . . . we may live" (Hos. 6:1–2); *Gk:* "faith . . . goodness . . . knowledge . . . self-control . . . perseverance . . . godliness . . . brotherly kindness . . . love" (2 Peter 1:5–7).

**CLUSTER.** Two or more consonants occurring initially or finally in a syllable. Initial clusters are rare in Hebrew but common in Greek; → digraph. *Heb: qāṭalt,* "she killed." *Gk: stauros,* "cross."

**CODEX (pl., CODICES).** An ancient → manuscript in book form, made of → papyrus, → parchment, or → vellum. In earlier times, documents were written on scrolls or clay tablets; the codex became dominant in the second century A.D. among Christian → scribes.

**CODEX ALEXANDRINUS.** An early-fifth-century A.D. → manuscript of the entire Bible in Greek. It was given by the Patriarch of Alexandria to King Charles I in 1627, hence its name. The → siglum A is used to denote this → codex.

**CODEX BEZAE.** A bilingual → manuscript, dated from the fourth to sixth centuries A.D., that contains Greek and Latin texts of the Gospels and Acts on facing pages. It is named for Theodore Bezae, who gave it to Cambridge University in 1581; it still remains in the library there. The → siglum D is used to denote this → codex.

**CODEX CAIRENSIS.** Another name for the → Cairo Prophets.

**CODEX CLAROMONTANUS.** A sixth-century A.D. Greco-Latin → manuscript of the Epistles of Paul.

**CODEX EPHRAEMI.** The remains of a fifth-century A.D. Greek → manuscript of the whole Bible. In the twelfth century it was separated and the 209 leaves that survive were erased and used to copy some writings of a fourth-century Syriac father named Ephraem. Therefore, technically this → codex is a → palimpsest. The → siglum C is used to denote this codex.

**CODEX KORIDETHI.** A ninth-century A.D. → codex that is the primary witness to the Caesarean text of Mark's Gospel. The → siglum θ is used to denote this codex.

**CODEX SINAITICUS.** A late-fourth-century A.D. Greek Bible with much of the OT missing, found in the monastery of St. Catherine at Mount Sinai. The → siglum א is used to denote this → codex.

**CODEX VATICANUS.** An early-fourth-century A.D. Greek Bible. The → siglum B is used to denote this → codex.

**CODEX WASHINGTON.** A fourth- or fifth-century A.D. → codex, acquired for the United States by C. L. Freer in 1906. The → siglum W is used to denote this codex.

**COGNATE.** Of common origin. *Ex:* Spanish and Portuguese are cognate languages; German *Vater* and English "father" are cognate words.

**COGNATE ACCUSATIVE.** A → noun, derived from the same → root as the → verb, that defines, explains, or strengthens (emphasizes) the verbal idea. It is also called the *absolute object,* the *internal object, schema etymologicum,* or *figura etymologica. Heb:* "Jerusalem has sinned greatly" (Lam. 1:8), lit., "Jerusalem has sinned a sin." *Gk:* "If anyone sees his brother commit a sin" (1 John 5:16), lit., "sinning a sin."

**COHESION/COHESIVE.** A term used to describe the way in which the various parts of a text are related to one another to reveal clearly the development or progression of the text.

**COHORTATIVE.** → Modal → aspect of a → verb, expressing desire, will, request, wish, self-encouragement, intention of the speaker for himself. It may be considered a modified → imperative and usually appears in the first

→ person. *Heb:* "Then God said, '*Let us make* man in our image'" (Gen. 1:26). *Gk:* "*Let us run* with perseverance the race marked out for us" (Heb. 12:1). Also called *hortatory.* → Optative, → Jussive, → Volitive.

**COLLATE/COLLATION.** In → textual criticism, this term refers to the compilation and critical comparison of → variant → manuscript readings of a given text in order to determine textual differences and thereby reconstruct the original text.

**COLLECTIVE NOUN.** A → noun that may be singular in form but designates a group as a unit (e.g., the *team* won *its* game); it is also a noun that may be considered plural when individuals are indicated (e.g., the *class* received *their* diplomas). *Heb:* "let them rule over the *fish* of the sea and the *birds* [lit., bird] of the air" (Gen. 1:26). *Gk:* "*Crowds* [lit., multitude] gathered also from the towns around Jerusalem" (Acts 5:16).

**COLLOQUIALISM.** A word or expression used in spoken and informal language rather than in written and formal language.

**COLOMETRY/COLOMETRIC.** The measurement and arrangement of a → manuscript in terms of sense or space lines, i.e., arranged by smaller units of → comma or → colon. *Ex:* Codex Bezae is written with thirty-three colometric lines per page.

**COLON (pl., COLA).** The basic thought unit in poetry, composed of two or more words, but rarely more than five. In Greek NT → manuscripts, a line of at least nine but no more than sixteen syllables. A line is made up of two cola (bicola) or three cola (tricola). → Stich, → Bistich, → Distich, → Hemistich, → Tristich, → Stanza.

**COLOPHON.** An inscription placed at the end of a document that gives information such as the author's name, place and date of publication, or a comment by the author.

**COLWELL'S RULE.** In Greek, definite → predicate → nouns that follow the → verb take the article; definite predicate nouns that precede the verb generally do not. *Gk:* "Surely this man was *the* Son of God" (Mark 15:39); *huios theou* precedes the verb *ēn* and is therefore → anarthrous.

**COMMA (pl., COMMATA).** A → manuscript line comprising a single → phrase; in Greek manuscripts, a combination of words not in excess of eight syllables.

**COMMENDATION, RECOMMENDATION.** A letter form in the Greco-Roman world, called *systatikē* in Greek, by which one introduced a friend to other acquaintances. *Gk:* "Or do we need, like some people, letters of recommendation to you or from you?" (2 Cor. 3:1; cf. Acts 18:27; Rom. 16:1).

**COMMENTARY.** A study of a book (or of several books) of the Bible that employs linguistic, critical, historical, and theological disciplines and insights. Some well-known commentaries are *The Interpreter's Bible, The International Critical Commentary,* and *The Expositor's Bible Commentary.*

**COMMON ERA.** → C. E.

**COMMON GENDER.** → Gender.

**COMMON NOUN.** → Noun.

**COMMUTATION.** A change in the consonant in the spelling of a word. In biblical languages, commutation usually represents the change from a harder to a softer sound, e g , from → aspirated to → smooth, although the pattern is hardly predictable. *Heb:* ṣāḥaq to šāḥaq. *Gk:* kreisson to kreitton. → Permutation.

**COMPAGINIS LETTERS.** In Hebrew, an ending on a word that reflects an obsolete case ending (î or ô).

**COMPARATIO DECURTATA.** The description of an external or internal state in the form of a comparison with some well-known class. *Heb:* "You are like a lion among the nations" (Ezek. 32:2). *Gk:* "Your enemy the devil prowls around like a roaring lion" (1 Peter 5:8).

**COMPARATIVE DEGREE.** Forms of → adjectives and → adverbs, or adjectival and adverbial constructions, that express relative increase of quality, quantity, or intensity. In English, the comparative degree is expressed by an adjective with the suffix -*er* (rich*er*) or by "more" with an adverb (*more* richly). In Hebrew, it is expressed by various means (the preposition *min* or the context); in Greek, by means of suffixes and certain particles. *Heb:* "God made . . . the *greater* light . . . and the *lesser* light" (Gen. 1:16). *Gk:* "After me will come one *more* powerful *than* I" (Mark 1:7).

**COMPARATIVE RELIGION.** A comparative historical and theological study of the various religions of the world with a particular interest in discovering their similarities and mutual relations.

**COMPENSATORY LENGTHENING.** The lengthening of a short vowel to make up for the loss of one or more consonants. *Heb:* instead of doubling a consonant, a preceding vowel may be lengthened in the formation of the *piel* stem before *aleph*, *ayin*, or *resh*, e.g., *bērah* for *birrah*. *Gk:* in the formation of the first aorist stem before *lambda*, *nu*, or *rho*, e.g., *emeina* for *emensa*.

**COMPLEMENT/COMPLEMENTARY.** In the broadest sense, a word, → phrase, or → clause that completes the meaning of a grammatical construction, especially the → predicate. *Ex:* a → direct object is a predicate complement. The term is restricted in some grammars to a complement following a → copula. → Subject Complement, → Object Complement.

**COMPLEXIVE AORIST.** Another name for a → constative aorist.

**COMPLEX SENTENCE.** A sentence composed of one → main clause plus at least one → subordinate clause. *Ex:* "When they heard this, they were amazed" (Matt. 22:22).

**COMPOSITE SHEWA.** A form of the → *shewa* in the Hebrew language that normally appears with → guttural letters. There are three composite *shewas:* ᵃ, ᵉ, and ᵒ. Also called *compound shewa.*

**COMPOSITION.** The art of putting together words and sentences in accordance with the rules of grammar and → rhetoric; in grammar, the relationship between → morpheme, word, → phrase, → clause, → sentence, and discourse.

**COMPOSITION CRITICISM.** An alternative term for → redaction criticism, used by some scholars to emphasize the compositional technique of a true author as opposed to a mere → redactor or editor.

**COMPOUND-COMPLEX SENTENCE.** A sentence composed of two or more → main clauses plus at least one → subordinate clause. *Ex:* "When Israel was a child, I loved him, and out of Egypt I called my son" (Hos. 11:1).

**COMPOUND CONSONANT.** → Double Consonant.

**COMPOUND SENTENCE.** A sentence composed of two or more → main clauses, often joined by a → coordinating → conjunction. *Ex:* "Gladness and joy will overtake them, and sorrow and sighing will flee away" (Isa. 35:10).

**COMPOUND SHEWA.** → Composite Shewa.

**COMPOUND WORD.** A word composed of two or more free → morphemes; the result of → agglutination, often employing a → preposition. *Ex:* English *bedroom. Heb:* ṣalmāweṯ, "shadow of death." *Gk: epiballō,* "to cast upon."

**CONATIVE.** An → aspect of the verb that indicates attempted action. *Gk:* "He *tried to reconcile* them" (Acts 7:26). → Desiderative.

**CONCESSIVE.** Expresses a concession ("although," "yet," "even if"), often in an → adverbial clause. *Heb:* "*Even if* you offer many prayers, I will not listen" (Isa. 1:15). *Gk:* "*Even if* I caused you sorrow by my letter, I do not regret it" (2 Cor. 7:8).

**CONCORD.** The grammatical harmony of → person, → gender, and → number among parts of the sentence and among units of → discourse; also called *agreement.* *Ex:* a pronoun in Hebrew and Greek agrees with its → antecedent in person, gender, and number.

**CONCORDANCE.** An alphabetical listing of the principal words in a book, giving all or some of the places where the word occurs. *Ex: Young's Analytical Concordance.*

**CONCRETE NOUN.** → Noun.

**CONDITION/CONDITIONAL CLAUSE.** A type of → adverbial clause that poses an "if"; also called a → *protasis.* There are four conditional sentence structures in Greek. *Heb:* "*If* my head were shaved, my strength would leave me" (Judg. 16:17). See also → *apodosis.*

**CONFESSIONAL FORMULA.** A stereotyped summary of the Christian faith; in the NT, especially in Paul's letters, a primitive creedal → formula acclaiming the lordship of Jesus Christ. *Gk:* "if you confess with your mouth, 'Jesus is Lord' " (Rom. 10:9; cf. Acts 17:7; 1 Cor. 12:3; Col. 2:6; Phil. 2:11). → Credo, → Homologia.

**CONFLATION.** A textual *variant* that arose from the mixture of two other variants; the result is an expanded text. Also a merging of two separated texts into one reading. Also called double reading, → *doublet,* or alternative reading.

**CONFLICT DIALOGUE.** → Controversy Dialogue.

**CONJ.** → Cj.

**CONJECTURE.** A reconstruction of a text or part of a text that is believed to represent the original, although there is no extant → manuscript that contains the proposed reconstruction.

**CONJUGATION.** An orderly arrangement or listing of the → inflected forms of a → verb or → verbal according to its → person, → gender, → number, → tense, → voice, and → mode.

**CONJUNCTION/CONJUNCTIVE.** A part of speech that joins words, → phrases, or → clauses together in a → coordinate or → subordinate construction and expresses a unity of idea. *Ex:* "And God said, 'Let there be light'" (Gen. 1:3). The term may also be used of an accent mark in Hebrew that is part of the system of → Masoretic accent marks known as *conjunctives* and → *disjunctives*. The conjunctive marks indicate a syntactical relationship between words. Some Greek grammars prefer the term → particle for subordinating conjunctions like *hina* and *hoti*.

**CONNECTING LINK.** → Connective.

**CONNECTIVE.** A connective is a word or → phrase that connects other words, phrases, → clauses, etc., in a → coordinate or → subordinate construction. *Heb:* "And [*waw*] God said, 'Let there be light'" (Gen. 1:3). *Gk:* "and [*kai*] nothing is to be rejected if it is received with thanksgiving" (1 Tim. 4:4). → Conjunction.

**CONNOTATIVE MEANING.** That aspect of meaning that concerns the emotive components of a word. → Denotative Meaning.

**CONSECUTIVE.** → Waw Consecutive.

**CONSECUTIVE CLAUSE.** Another name for a → result clause.

**CONSONANT.** A speech sound made by narrowing the breath channel sufficiently to cause audible friction or by restricting some other part of the breath passage. There are twenty-two consonants in Hebrew and seventeen in Greek. They are commonly divided into → mutes (stops), → spirants, → liquids, → nasals, and → double (compound) consonants. For names and pronunciation of the Hebrew and Greek consonants, see *Gesenius' Hebrew Grammar* (Kautzsch-Cowley 2nd ed.), sections 5–6; and Robertson's *New Short Grammar of the Greek Testament*, sections 34–41. → Vowel.

**CONSTATIVE AORIST.** The basic use of the → aorist tense in → narrative to summarize an activity or series of events over a period of time. Also called *global, summary,* or *complexive*. *Gk:* "Nevertheless, death *reigned* from the time of Adam to the time of Moses" (Rom. 5:14).

**CONSTRUCTIO AD SENSUM.** → Ad Sensum.

**CONSTRUCTION.** The systematic arrangement of the various parts of speech into → phrases, → clauses, and → sentences. Also called *structure.*

**CONSTRUCTIO PRAEGNANS.** → Pregnant Construction.

**CONSTRUCT STATE.** A word in Hebrew that is dependent on the following word for meaning and definiteness (also for → accent if the words are joined by a → *maqqeph*); together they make up a compound state that is the equivalent of the → genitive in English or Greek. It is also called → *annexion. Heb:* "God set them in the expanse of [construct] the sky" (Gen. 1:17). → Absolute State.

**CONSUMMATIVE.** An → aspect of the verb that depicts the completion or result of the action (or state). A basic force of the → *perfect* tense. *Gk:* "Yet you *have filled* Jerusalem with your teaching" (Acts 5:28).

**CONTEXT.** The larger portion of Scripture in which a passage or verse appears; consideration of context is important for correct interpretation.

**CONTINUANTS.** Another name for → spirants.

**CONTROVERSY DIALOGUE.** A subcategory of → apothegm; a brief → narrative context containing a pronouncement of Jesus in reply to adversaries, generally on the issues of Jewish law. *Gk:* Mark 2:1–12; 3:1–5; 12:13–17. Also called *conflict dialogue.*

**CONVERSIVE.** → Waw Consecutive.

**COORDINATE/COORDINATION.** The linking of grammatical units of equal rank. Coordinate → clauses occur in a → compound sentence; they can be joined by a coordinating → conjunction such as *or, but,* or *and.* → Parataxis.

**COPTIC.** The language used by early Christians in Egypt. It developed from the ancient Egyptian language. Portions of the Bible are extant in six Coptic dialects: Sahidic, Bohairic, Achmimic, sub-Achmimic, Middle Egyptian, and Fayyumic.

**COPULA/COPULATIVE.** A linking word, such as *and* or the verb *to be.* The Greek copula (usually *eimi* or *ginomai*) links the → subject and the → complement, which are both in the → nominative case. The copula is often omitted (→ ellipsis). Also called *linking verb, equative verb,* and *verb of being.*

**COPULATIVE WAW.** → Waw Conjunctive.

**COPYIST.** In biblical studies, one who copies the Scriptures. → Scribe.

**CORONIS.** A → diacritical mark (') used to indicate → crasis in Greek; it is placed over the contracted syllable. *Gk: kâgō*, "I also." → Apostrophe.

**CORPUS HERMETICUM.** → Hermetic Literature.

**CORRELATIVE.** A → conjunction used in a grammatical construction as one of a pair that correlates words, → phrases, or → clauses. *Ex: both . . . and, just as . . . even so.* *Heb: "Neither* curse them at all *nor* bless them at all!" (Num. 23:25). *Gk: "As* the Father has loved me, *so* have I loved you" (John 15:9).

**COSMOGONY.** A theory regarding the creation and origination of the world or universe.

**COSMOLOGY.** Study of the orderly system or character of the universe. The ancient Near East largely conceived of a three-tiered cosmology: the earth, the water below, and the heavens above.

**COUPLET.** Another name for a → distich.

**CRASIS.** In Greek, the contraction of a → vowel or → diphthong at the end of a word with one at the beginning of the following word; with a few exceptions, crasis is found in constructions with *kai.* The contraction is indicated by a → coronis. *Gk: kâgō = kai* ("and") + *egō* ("I"), "I also." → Apostrophe.

**CREDO.** A creed or brief, authoritative expression of religious beliefs. Gerhard von Rad argued that such passages as Deut. 6:20–24, 26:5b–9, and Josh. 24:2b–13 are creeds of the faith of ancient Israel.

**CREEDAL.** Of, or pertaining to, a creed or → credo.

**CRITICAL APPARATUS.** The textual critical footnotes found in Hebrew and Greek editions of the OT and NT. These notes supply → readings that support or differ from the printed text and give → manuscript sources for comparative studies of the text.

**CRITICAL TEXT.** A hypothetical reconstruction of a document based on available divergent → recensions.

**CRITICISM.** A general term that refers to analysis of the Scriptures. There are many kinds of critical studies; see the following: biblical criticism, canonical criticism, form criticism, grammatico-historical criticism, higher criticism, historical criticism, literary criticism, Pentateuchal criticism, redaction criticism, religio-historical criticism, rhetorical criticism, source criticism, structural analysis, stylistic criticism, textual (lower) criticism, and tradition criticism.

**CRUX INTERPRETUM.** A Latin term for the major point at issue; the heart of the matter in the interpretation of a difficult passage.

**CRYPTOGRAM.** A writing that has sacred or hidden meaning; also a drawing that has hidden or symbolic meaning. *Heb:* "Sheshach" for Babylon (Jer. 25:26). *Gk:* "Babylon" for Rome (1 Peter 5:13).

**CULMINATIVE AORIST.** Another name for → effective aorist.

**CULT/CULTIC.** The public worship practices of a people, involving established forms, rites, feasts, times, places, etc. When used in biblical studies, the word should not be confused with its popular connotation (Satan cult, etc.).

**CUNEIFORM.** Wedge-shaped script written with a sharp instrument on tablets of soft clay, which were then baked, or carved on stone. This method of writing was used by the Sumerians, Akkadians, Babylonians, Assyrians, and other ancient Near Eastern peoples.

**CURSIVE.** Letters joined together one after another with strokes; also called → minuscule writing. → Majuscule.

**CUSTOMARY.** → Iterative.

**D.** Abbreviation of Deuteronomic Source, used by many OT scholars to identify the scroll found in the temple in 622 B.C. during the reforms of Josiah because of the belief that this scroll was the Book of Deuteronomy or some portion of it. → JEDP.

**DAGHESH FORTE.** A dot that may appear in all the Hebrew consonants except the → gutturals. It doubles the consonant in which it appears.

**DAGHESH FORTE DIRIMENS.** A consonant with → *shewa* is strengthened by *daghesh forte dirimens* to make the *shewa* more audible (e.g., ʿinneḇê).

**DAGHESH FORTE IMPLICITUM.** *Daghesh forte* is omitted (as in *he* or *heth*), but strengthening is considered to have taken place; the *daghesh forte* is implied. It is also called *occultum* or *delitescens*.

**DAGHESH LENE.** A dot that appears only in the → *begad kephat* letters in Hebrew. It affects the pronunciation by giving the consonant in which it appears a hard sound.

**DATIVE CASE.** In Greek, the → case of personal interest used to express, among other relationships, the indirect object. There is no dative case in Hebrew, but there are various ways of expressing the dative idea. *Gk:*

"Jesus spoke all these things *to the crowd* in parables" (Matt. 13:34).

**DATIVE OF ADVANTAGE/DATIVE OF DISADVANTAGE.** → Dativus Commodi/Dativus Incommodi.

**DATIVUS COMMODI/DATIVUS INCOMMODI.** Latin terms for → dative of advantage and disadvantage; in Greek, a root idea of the dative case, designating the person whose interest is affected. *Gk:* "it is *for the sake of* God . . . it is *for* you" (2 Cor. 5:13). → Ethical Dative.

**DATIVUS ETHICUS.** → Ethical Dative.

**DAUGHTER TRANSLATION.** A translation of the → Septuagint into another language.

**DEAD SEA SCROLLS.** Writings of an Essene community that were discovered in 1947 near the Dead Sea. They have been dated between 168 B.C. and A.D. 233. They include the oldest OT manuscripts yet discovered.

**DECALOGUE.** From Greek, "ten words." Another name for the Ten Commandments (Exod. 20:1–17; Deut. 5:6–21).

**DECLENSION.** An orderly arrangement or listing of the → inflection of a → noun, → pronoun, → participle, or → adjective according to its → case, → person, → gender, and → number.

**DEDUCTIVE METHOD.** The process of reasoning from the general to the particular, as opposed to inductive, which goes from the particular to the general. For biblical languages, a traditional method of pedagogy and grammar that introduces the learner to grammatical structure by rules and → paradigms and then applies the principles learned to the reading of texts. By contrast, the inductive method begins with the text and leads the student to formulate grammatical structure by generalizing from examples encountered in reading.

**DEFECTIVE VERB.** A verb whose → conjugation is not complete, usually requiring the substitution of an entirely different stem (→ suppletion). *Ex: go, went, gone. Heb:* ṭôḇ, "to be good," in the perfect; *yîṭaḇ* in the imperfect. *Gk: legō,* "I say," in the present; *eipon,* "I said," in the aorist.

**DEFECTIVE WRITING.** When the → vowel letter is omitted in Hebrew. Also called *scriptio defectiva. Ex:* the writing of ō for ô. → Plena.

**DEFINITE.** → Determinate.

**DELIBERATIVE.** An → aspect of the verb that poses a questioning state of mind; → rhetorical question. In the Greek → future tense or → subjunctive mood, a question not about facts but about the possibility, desirability, or necessity of a proposed course of action. *Gk:* "Lord, to whom shall we go?" (John 6:28). → Desiderative.

**DELTA TEXT.** Another name for the → Western text.

**DEMONSTRATIVE ADJECTIVE.** An adjective that points out particular persons, places, or things. There are two types: near (*this, these*) and remote (*that, those*). The demonstrative adjective is also called a demonstrative pronoun.

**DEMONSTRATIVE PRONOUN.** → Demonstrative Adjective.

**DEMOTIC.** A simplified form of → hieratic, written from right to left. Also refers to the modern Greek → vernacular.

**DEMYTHOLOGIZE.** To interpret those parts of the Bible considered to be mythological (i.e., where the supernatural, transcendent is described in terms of the mundane, this-worldly) by understanding the essential existential truths contained in the imagery of the myth.

Rudolf Bultmann is particularly associated with de-mythologizing the Scriptures.

**DENOMINAL.** → Denominative.

**DENOMINATIVE.** A noun or a verb derived from a noun or adjective → stem. *Heb: šōʿēr,* "porter," from *šaʿar,* "gate"; *Gk: grammateus,* "scribe," from *gramma,* "letter." Also called *denominal.*

**DENOTATIVE MEANING.** The aspect of meaning that most closely relates to that portion of the nonlinguistic world to which the word refers. Also called *referential meaning. Ex:* the denotative meaning of "father" includes *human, male, generation,* and *ancestor,* whereas the → connotative meaning suggests *care, love, protection,* and *discipline.*

**DENTAL.** The → mute consonants whose sounds are produced by the tongue against the teeth. The dentals in Hebrew are *daleth, tet,* and *taw;* in Greek they are *delta, theta,* and *tau.* Also called *linguals.*

**DEPENDENT CLAUSE.** Another name for a → subordinate clause.

**DEPONENT.** From Latin *deponere,* "to lay aside [the active form]." In Greek, a → verb or → verbal that has a middle-passive form (also its → lexical form) but an active meaning. *Gk: erchomai,* "I come, go."

**DERIVATION.** Addition of → affixes to a → stem to derive a new word, in contrast to → inflection, which produces another form of the same word. For derived forms in Hebrew and Greek see → demoninative and → deverbative.

**DESIDERATIVE.** Expressing a wish or desire to perform the action denoted by the verb. Also called → *optative.* → Conative, → Subjunctive Mood.

**DETERMINATE.** A word that is definite by its very nature (e.g., a proper name) or made definite by composition or → syntax. In Hebrew, a word → prefixed with an article or with a pronominal → suffix → affixed, or a → construct followed by a definite → absolute word becomes determinate. In Greek, a word is made definite by the article, or, in the case of predicate nouns, by the position before the verb. Also called *definite*. → Colwell's Rule.

**DEUS EX MACHINA.** Latin for "god out of the machine." In Greek drama a deity was lowered suddenly onto the stage by mechanical means to resolve the dilemma at hand or untangle the plot. The phrase is now applied pejoratively to contrived solutions by means of an artificial or improbable device.

**DEUTEROCANON/DEUTEROCANONICAL.** A term used by Roman Catholics to designate books or parts of books that are not found in the Hebrew Bible but are included in the → Septuagint and accepted as inspired since the Council of Trent; others call these books the → Apocrypha. The Catholics refer to the → Pseudepigrapha as the Apocrypha.

**DEUTEROGRAPH.** A term used to express the relationship of certain texts to each other or the repetitive nature of the subject matter of certain Scriptures. *Ex:* 1 Chron. 10–2 Chron. 36 are deuterographs of 1 Sam. 31–2 Kings 25; Exod. 20:1–17 and Deut. 5:6–21; 2 Peter 2 and Jude.

**DEUTERO-ISAIAH.** The name given to the unknown author of Isaiah 40–55 (sometimes applied to Isaiah 40–66) by those who do not accept the unity of the Book of Isaiah. → Trito-Isaiah.

**DEUTERONOMIST HISTORIAN.** A designation given by many scholars to an unknown editor responsible for compiling the books of Deuteronomy, Joshua, Judges, 1–2 Samuel, and 1–2 Kings, ca. 550 B.C.

**DEUTERO-PAULINE.** Name given to canonical letters of Paul whose authenticity is doubted by some scholars; usually ascribed to the work of a Pauline admirer who imitated the apostle's style. The list includes Ephesians, Colossians, 2 Thessalonians, 1–2 Timothy, and Titus.

**DEUTERO-ZECHARIAH.** The name given to the unknown author of Zechariah 9–11 by those who do not accept the unity of Zechariah. → Trito-Zechariah.

**DEVERBAL.** → Deverbative.

**DEVERBATIVE.** A noun or verb derived from a verb → stem. *Heb: memšelet,* "dominion," from *mšl,* "to rule." *Gk: logos,* "word," from *legō,* "I say." Also called *deverbal.*

**DIACHRONIC.** From Greek, "through time." A term used to refer to the evolutionary or changing state of a language over a period of time. *Heb: ylk* became *hlk; Gk:* the dual number was dropped. → Synchronic.

**DIACRITICAL MARK/DIACRITICAL POINT.** A mark or sign attached to a letter to distinguish it in form or sound; in Hebrew grammar also called → *puncta extraordinaria.*

**DIALECT.** One of a number of varieties of a language, especially as differentiated by geographical region or by social class. *Ex:* Ugaritic, Hebrew, and Aramaic are northwest Semitic dialects; Ionic, Doric, and Attic are classical Greek dialects.

**DIALOGUE.** A conversation between two or more persons. The character of biblical faith—the relationship of God and man—makes dialogue an inevitable form of rhetorical expression. *Heb:* "Come now, let us reason together" (Isa. 1:18); Hab. 1–2 contains a dialogue between God and the prophet. *Gk:* "Then one of the elders asked me . . . I answered" (Rev. 7:13–14).

**DIARESIS.** A → diacritical mark (¨) placed over the second of two vowels to indicate that they are not pronounced as a → diphthong; in Greek, over *i* or *u*. *Gk: Ioudaïsmos*, "Judaism."

**DIASPORA.** The dispersion or scattering of the Jewish people after the Exile of 587 B.C., particularly the extended settlements following the conquests of Alexander the Great.

**DIATESSARON.** Greek "through four." The → harmony of the four Gospels compiled by Tatian of Syria, ca. A.D. 150–160; this composite gospel was the standard text in → Syriac-speaking churches until the fifth century; it survives only in fragments.

**DIATRIBE.** A prolonged bitter, abusive harangue. As a Greco-Roman literary → genre, it has been compared to portions of Paul's letters, e.g., Romans 1–3.

**DICTATION THEORY.** The belief that God "dictated" the Bible to its authors, thus bypassing any human involvement beyond the writing down of the words. → Verbal Inspiration.

**DIDACHE.** Greek for "teaching." A technical term for teaching or catechetical material in the apostolic tradition in contrast to → kerygma. Early preaching, however, clearly combined the two emphases. *Ex:* ethical teaching given during the evangelization of Thessalonica (1 Thess. 4:1–2).

**DIDACTIC.** That which is intended to teach or instruct. Much of the OT and NT is didactic in nature. *Ex:* the Sermon on the Mount.

**DIGLOT.** An edition of the biblical text with a translation in a parallel column or on the facing page. Greek-Latin diglots of the NT date from the fifth century A.D., the most famous being → Codex Bezae.

**DIGRAPH.** Two successive letters whose phonetic value is a single, changed sound or that are written as a single letter. *Gk: gg* is pronounced like *ng* in *finger;* the written digraphs are *zeta, xi,* and *psi.* → Cluster, → Double Consonants.

**DIMINUTIVE.** A word formed with an → affix meaning small or little, used literally or metaphorically as a term of affection; also called → *hypocoristicon. Ex: droplet. Gk: teknon,* "child," *teknion,* "little child"; "And now, *dear children [teknia],* continue in him" (1 John 2:28).

**DIPHTHONG.** A speech sound composed of two vowel sounds but pronounced as one. *Ex: ai, oi.* → Monophthong.

**DIRECT ADDRESS.** The use of a noun or pronoun to name the person or thing spoken to. *Heb:* "*Queen Esther,* what is your petition?" (Esth. 7:2). *Gk:* "Woe to you, *Bethsaida!*" (Luke 10:13); when used rhetorically, as in this example, direct address becomes → apostrophe. → Direct Discourse.

**DIRECT CASES.** → Oblique Cases.

**DIRECT DISCOURSE.** The exact words of a speaker reported directly in narrative discourse; in English it is indicated by quotation marks. *Heb:* "Then David said to the whole assembly, '*Praise the* LORD *your God*'" (1 Chron. 29:20); *Gk:* "Then Jesus asked him, '*What is your name?*'" (Mark 5:9). Also called *oratio recta.*

**DIRECT EQUIVALENCE.** A theory of translation that believes only one English word should be used to represent each Hebrew or Greek word found in the OT and NT. → Metaphrase, → Formal Correspondence.

**DIRECT OBJECT.** The word, → phrase, or → clause that is the primary goal or result of the action of the verb (cf. → accusative case); the person or thing is directly affected by the action of the verb. *Heb:* "God created the *heavens* and the *earth*" (Gen. 1:1). *Gr:* "He grabbed *him* and began to choke *him*" (Matt. 18:28).

**DIRGE.** A composition, either musical or literary, that expresses grief. *Ex:* Lam. 1.

**DISCIPLINA ARCANI.** Latin for "discipline of the secret." The practice ascribed to the early church of concealing the mysteries of the faith and certain religious observances from new converts and pagans.

**DISCOURSE.** A biblical passage displaying semantic and structural coherence, unity, and completeness, and conveying a message. From a linguistic viewpoint, discourse is marked by certain universals or restraints that give it structure. *Ex:* the Bread of Life discourse (John 6:25–59). → Discourse Analysis.

**DISCOURSE ANALYSIS.** The linguistic task of discovering the regular features of discourse structure, the way in which words, → phrases, → clauses, and especially sentences and whole → compositions are joined to achieve a given purpose.

**DISJUNCTIVE.** A part of speech that joins words that are in co-ordinate construction and expresses a contrast between their ideas. *Ex: but, or.* The term may also be used of an accent mark in Hebrew that is part of the system of → Masoretic accent marks known as → *conjunctives* and *disjunctives.* The disjunctive marks indicate separation between word relationships.

**DISSIMILATION.** The process by which two adjacent sounds of similar quality become dissimilar; the opposite of → assimilation. It is not characteristic of Hebrew but occurs regularly in Greek. *Gk:* a → *dental* mute before another dental becomes *sigma: pepeithtai* becomes *pepeistai.*

**DISTICH.** A larger poetic unit that is composed of two lines; also called *couplet.* → Colon.

**DISTRIBUTIVE.** A word that expresses separation among individuals or groups. *Ex: each, every.* Grammatical function answering the question, "How many each?"

**DITTOGRAPHY.** The accidental writing twice of a letter, letters, a word, or a phrase that should only have been written once. → Haplography.

**DIVINATION.** The use of various means (such as examination of livers) to determine future events or the will of a deity. Various kinds of divination (including technical terms) are discussed in William W. Hallo and William K. Simpson, *The Ancient Near East*, pp. 158–63; and John L. McKenzie, *A Theology of the Old Testament*, p. 68.

**DOCETISM/DOCETIC.** From Greek *dokein*, "to seem." A christological heresy of → Gnosticism, which asserted that Christ "seemed" to suffer, i.e., the death of the divine Christ was only apparent, not real. *Ex:* docetism is the target of the polemic in 1 John 5:6.

**DOCUMENTARY HYPOTHESIS.** A theory that explains the formation of the Scriptures, especially the → Pentateuch, as being the result of combining a number of documents from different sources. → Source Criticism, → JEDP.

**DOMINICAL SAYING.** A saying of the Lord (Latin, *dominus*); a saying of Jesus recorded in the Gospels. → Logion.

**DOUAY BIBLE.** Name of the first Catholic version of the Bible in the English language, translated from the → Vulgate in 1609. Also called *Douai-Rheims Bible.*

**DOUBLE CONSONANTS.** In Greek, the consonant letters that represent the combination of a → mute with *sigma*; also called *compound consonants*. The written forms (→ digraph) are *xi* for *ks, gs,* and *chs; psi* for *ps, bs,* and *phs; zeta* for *ds.*

**DOUBLE DUTY MODIFIER, DOUBLE DUTY WORD.** A literary device in which a word or → phrase can be understood to be part of what precedes or of what follows. *Heb:* the phrase "with all my heart" in Ps. 86:12; the verb in "God made two great lights" (Gen. 1:16 KJV) serves double duty with the phrase "the stars also" in the same verse. *Gk:* "in love" with "blameless in his sight" or "he predestined" (Eph. 1:4).

**DOUBLE READING.** Another name for → doublet. → Conflation.

**DOUBLET.** Two words in a language that are derived from the same original word. *Ex: guard, ward.* Two parallel lines of a literary composition. Also, two biblical narratives considered to be derived from the same original source. *Ex:* 1 Sam. 24 and 26; Mark 6:30–44 and 8:1–10. Also called *double reading, alternative reading,* or → *conflation.*

**DOUBLE TRADITION.** The common material of any two → Synoptic Gospels that is not found in the third; the term usually refers to the common material of Matthew and Luke not found in Mark (→ Q). The phrase does not presuppose any source hypothesis. → Source Criticism.

**DOXOLOGY.** From Greek *doxa,* "praise," "glory." An ascription of praise or glory to God or the persons of the Trinity, usually found at the end of a literary section. *Heb:* "Praise be to the LORD, the God of Israel, from everlasting to everlasting" (1 Chron. 16:36). *Gk:* "Oh, the depth of the riches of the wisdom and knowledge of God!" (Rom. 11:33).

**DSS.** Abbreviation of → Dead Sea Scrolls.

**DUALISM.** Any doctrine that asserts that there are two absolute powers or principles. Matter and spirit in → Gnosticism are two ultimately opposed realms of being; biblical dualism is ethical in character, e.g., spirit versus flesh.

**DUAL NUMBER.** A form denoting two persons or things. The dual → suffix *-ayim* occurs in a few Hebrew nouns, but the Greek dual disappeared from use before the NT. *Heb: yôm,* "day," *yômayim,* "two days"; *yāḏ,* "hand," *yāḏayim,* "(two) hands."

**DURATIVE.** Another name for → linear.

**DYNAMIC EQUIVALENCE.** A type of translation in which the message of the biblical text is conveyed to the reader with effect equivalent to that for the original reader; closer to a → paraphrase, and contrasted with → formal equivalence.

**DYSTELEOLOGY.** The apparent absence of intelligent purpose in life or nature; sometimes the term is applied to floods, plagues, etc.

*E*

**E.** Abbreviation of → Elohist. → JEDP.

**EARLY CATHOLICISM.** Features of second-century catholicism that are said by some scholars to be found in the NT, especially the concepts of faith as a creed and the church as a saving institution. Used pejoratively in contrast to the principle of justification by faith.

**'EBED YAHWEH.** Hebrew for "The servant of the Lord."

**EBLA.** The ancient site in northwestern Syria of a major civilization around 2400–2250 B.C., whose archaeological finds were first announced publicly in 1976. They are being compared in importance to the → Dead Sea Scrolls.

**ECBATIC CLAUSE.** Another name for a → result clause.

**ECLECTICISM.** In → textual criticism, the approach that rejects the notion that any single → manuscript, → family, or → text-type is to be preferred; it rather evaluates → variant readings entirely on the basis of intrinsic probability or internal criteria. Also called *rational criticism.*

**EDITIO PRINCEPS.** Latin term for the first printed edition of an ancient text.

**EFFECTIVE AORIST.** A use of the → aorist tense in → narrative to emphasize the completion or culmination of an action or state. *Gk:* "You *have not lied* to men but to God" (Acts 5:4). Also called *perfective, resultative,* or *culminative.*

**EGYPTIAN TEXT.** Another name for the → Alexandrian text.

**EIGHTEEN BENEDICTIONS.** Hebrew, *Shemoneh Esreh,* the principal daily prayer of Judaism, comprising eighteen blessings of praise, petition, and thanksgiving. Some elements date to the → Second Temple period; the → anathema upon heretics (*birkat haminim*), probably against Jewish Christians, was added after the destruction of Jerusalem. Also called *Amidah,* "standing," because it is recited while standing.

**EISEGESIS.** Reading into a passage of Scripture the meaning one wants to find in it. → Exegesis.

**EKKLESIA.** Greek for "church" or "assembly."

**EL.** A Hebrew name for God in the OT. The word is the most general designation for deity and was also used by the Canaanites for the name of their chief god. Frequently combined with an adjective to create a name for God that expresses one of His attributes. → El Elyon, → El Olam, → El Shaddai.

**ELATIVE.** A special form or use of the → adjective or → adverb to express a very high degree of quality without the notion of comparison expressed by the → comparative and → superlative; it is found in Arabic and Greek. The majority of superlative forms in the NT have an elative sense, i.e., "very" or "exceedingly." *Gk:* "A very large crowd" (Matt. 21:8); "his very great and precious promises" (2 Peter 1:4).

**EL ELYON.** A name of God, customarily translated as "God Most High." The name occurs thirty-one times in the OT (e.g., Gen. 14:18). → El, → Elyon.

**ELIDE.** To omit or be omitted in → elision.

**ELISION.** The omission of parts of words or the cutting off, especially of a vowel, for the sake of → meter or → euphony (cf. → syncope); consonants may also elide. *Ex:* 'gainst for *against*. *Heb: mûm* for *meʾûm. Gk:* the dropping of a final short vowel before an initial vowel: *apʾ archēs* for *apo archēs.* The elided vowel is marked by an → apostrophe.

**ELLIPSIS.** Omission of a word or words, obviously understood but necessary to make the expression grammatically complete. Certain specifications of measure, weight, or time are commonly omitted after numerals in Hebrew: "a thousand [shekels] of silver" (Gen. 20:16); also Ps. 135:16–17. Omission of the → copula is common in Hebrew and Greek. *Heb:* "God saw that the light was good" (Gen. 1:4), lit., "God saw the light that good." *Gk:* "God is our witness" (1 Thess. 2:5), lit., "God witness."

**ELOAH.** A Hebrew name for God found 53 times in the OT, especially in the Book of Job (42 times). In addition to being a proper name of God, it can also refer to a god. → Elohim.

**ELOHIM.** A Hebrew name for God found 2570 times in the OT. It is the plural of → Eloah. In addition to being a proper name of God, it can also refer to gods in general. → El.

**ELOHIST.** In → source criticism, the name given to the person believed to be the author of the second oldest stratum of material in the → Pentateuch. This material is also called → *E.* → JEDP.

**EL OLAM.** A name of God, customarily translated as "Everlasting God." It occurs only a few times in the OT (e.g., Isa. 40:28). → El.

**EL SHADDAI.** A name of God, customarily translated as

"God Almighty." The name occurs forty-eight times in the OT (e.g., Exod. 6:3). → El, → Shaddai.

**ELYON.** A Hebrew name for God in the OT. It is usually combined with *El* and translated as "Most High God" or "God Most High" (e.g., Gen. 14:18; Ps. 57:2). → El, → El Elyon.

**EMBLEMATIC PARALLELISM.** In Hebrew poetry, one line of a couplet makes a literal statement, the other repeats it in the form of a figure (such as a → metaphor or → simile). *Ex:* Ps. 42:1.

**EMEND/EMENDATION.** A correction made in a text to improve the → reading of a difficult word or passage; it may or may not have the support of textual → variants.

**EMPHASIS.** Special importance given to one or more syllables or words by various means. *Heb:* emphasis may be expressed in a number of ways, such as reversal of normal word order, repetition of words, verbal → stems such as the → piel. *Gk:* emphasis may be expressed in a number of ways, such as reversal of normal word order, personal → pronouns, use of the → periphrastic verb form.

**EMPHATIC HE.** → Paragogic.

**ENALLAGE.** The exchange of one grammatical form for another. Enallage of → gender is the weakening of precise distinction between masculine, feminine, and neuter, so that → suffixes of one gender can frequently be used to refer to words of another gender. It is quite common in Hebrew, less so in Greek. *Heb:* "May the LORD show kindness to *you*" (Ruth 1:9); the pronoun is masculine though Naomi is speaking to her daughters-in-law. *Gk:* "They saw the man who had been possessed by *the legion* of demons" (Mark 5:15); masculine article although the word is feminine.

**ENCLITIC.** In Greek, a word so closely linked to a preceding word as to have, under certain conditions, no separate accent of its own. Enclitics include forms of the → pronoun, some → particles and → adverbs, and the verbs *eimi* and *phēmi*. *Gk: adelphōn sou,* "your brothers."

**ENCLITIC MEM.** In Hebrew, a *mem* written at the end of a word and as part of it without a word divider between; its function is uncertain. *Ex: lᵉ'addîrîm 'ām* (Judg. 5:13).

**ENCOMIUM.** From Greek, "revel." A laudatory discourse; in the Greco-Roman world sometimes the serious study of a person (→ bios) but more often a sophistic display. The → genre has been applied to the literary study of the Gospels.

**ENCYCLICAL.** A circular letter sent to all the churches in a given area; likely NT examples are Ephesians and 1 Peter.

**ENDZEIT.** German for "end-time." → Eschaton.

**ENERGIC *NUN*.** A verbal form in Hebrew that is strengthened by the insertion of a connecting *nun* between the verbal → stem and the → suffix. Also called *nun energicum, nun demonstrativum, nun epentheticum, epenthetic nun.*

**ENJAMBMENT.** In poetry, the running over of a sentence or thought from one line into another; the result is that closely related words fall in different lines. It is not too common in Hebrew. *Heb:* Isa. 11:9b; Zeph. 3:19.

**ENNEATEUCH.** Name given to the first nine books of the OT (counting 1–2 Samuel and 1–2 Kings each as one book and omitting Ruth).

**ENTMYTHOLOGISIERUNG.** The German term for → demythologizing.

**ENUMERATIO.** Latin, "enumeration." → Merismus.

**EPANADIPLOSIS.** Another name for → anaphora.

**EPANAPHORA.** Another name for → anaphora.

**EPANASTROPHE.** A type of → paronomasia in which the final syllable of a Hebrew word is reproduced in the word that immediately follows. Heb: *beḥēmāh hēm-māh,* "they are like the animals" (Eccl. 3:18).

**EPENTHESIS.** Insertion of a vowel or consonant into a word, particularly in the → inflection of the verb.

**EPENTHETIC NUN.** → Energic Nun.

**EPEXEGESIS/EPEXEGETICAL.** Grammatical functions that are explanatory. A noun that may have the force of an adjective; a formal → genitive; also called *explicative* or *explanatory. Ex:* a foolish man, lit., a fool of a man. In Greek, the epexegetical function regularly occurs with the infinitive and the conjunctions *kai* and *hina.*

**EPICENE NOUN.** A noun in which the distinction of sex may be neglected, all examples of a species being included under one gender, either masculine or feminine. *Heb:* "birds" (Gen. 1:20). *Gk: alōpēx,* "fox" (a feminine noun, used in Luke 13:32 to refer to Herod).

**EPIDEICTIC ORATORY.** The oratory of display prominent in the → Second Sophistic, where more attention is given to form than to content. → Panegyric.

**EPIDIORTHOSIS.** A rhetorical figure that makes subsequent correction of a previous statement that might have offended. *Gk:* "I have made a fool of myself, but you drove me to it" (2 Cor. 12:11).

**EPIGRAM/EPIGRAMMATIC.** A short poem that states concisely (and sometimes satirically) a single thought; any clever or witty thought that is expressed concisely and cleverly. *Heb:* Jer. 31:29. *Gk:* Matt. 23:24.

**EPIGRAPHY.** The study of → inscriptions written on durable materials such as stone.

**EPINICION.** A song composed to celebrate a victory (e.g., in war or in athletic competition). *Heb:* Judg. 5. *Gk:* Rev. 19.

**EPIPHANY.** A manifestation of God (Exod. 3, 19; Isa. 6; Ezek. 1); also called → *theophany.* Also, a feast celebrated on January 6 that commemorates the coming of the Magi as being the first manifestation of Jesus Christ to the Gentiles.

**EPIPHORA.** The repetition of a word, → phrase, or sound at the end of two or more verse lines, sentences, or → strophes in sequence. Also called *antistrophe. Heb:* "His love endures forever" (Ps. 136). *Gk:* "under the law" (1 Cor. 9:20). → Anaphora.

**EPISTLE.** Greek for "letter." A → genre of Greco-Roman public correspondence applied to the NT letters; now distinguished from the latter as a technical term in → literary criticism. → Letter.

**EPISTOLARY.** Of, or pertaining to, an → epistle.

**EPISTOLOGRAPHY.** The study of Hebrew and Greek → letter writing.

**EPITHALAMION.** A song or literary composition written to honor a bride or groom. *Ex:* Ps. 45.

**EPONYM.** One whose name is so prominently connected with something as to be a figurative designation for it. *Ex:* Israel, Judah.

**EQUATIVE VERB.** Another name for → copula.

**ESCHATOLOGY.** Strictly speaking, the study of events associated with the end of time; the term is drastically modified by some interpreters.

**ESCHATON.** Greek for "the end," i.e., of the present world order.

**ETHICAL DATIVE.** Used with verbs in order to give emphasis to the significance of the occurrence in question for a particular subject. *Heb: lek $l^e\underline{k}\bar{a}$,* lit., "go, to you" = "go away"; used mostly with imperatives. *Gk: ti hēmin,* lit., "what, to us" = "What do you want with us" (Mark 1:24). Also called *dativus ethicus.*

**ETHICAL LISTS.** Catalogs of vices or virtues used by NT writers in the context of → paraenesis; the literary forms are similar to those found in intertestamental Judaism and Greek Stoicism. *Ex:* catalogs of virtues (Gal. 5:22–23; 2 Cor. 6:6; Eph. 4:32–5:2; 1 Peter 3:8); catalogs of vices (Rom. 1:29–31; 1 Cor. 5:10–11; Gal. 5:19–21).

**ETHNICA.** Another name for → gentilic.

**ETIOLOGY, AETIOLOGY.** The study of causation. In biblical studies, a story or → narrative told to explain the circumstances surrounding the origin of an institution, custom, name, etc. *Ex:* Exod. 12 explains the origin of Passover, the Book of Esther the origin of the feast of Purim.

**ETYMOLOGY.** Study of the origin or derivation of a word.

**EUPHEMISM.** The substitution of an inoffensive or mild expression for one that may offend or be unpleasant. *Heb:* "feet" is sometimes used as an euphemism for the genitals (cf. 1 Sam. 24:3 KJV). *Gk:* "beds" for sexual immorality (cf. Rom. 13:13 KJV).

**EUPHONIC NUN.** A *nun* placed at the end of a Hebrew word for pleasing sound or ease of pronunciation. → Paragogic.

**EUPHONY.** Words or letters placed together because of their pleasing sound quality or ease of pronunciation. *Ex:* "*a* dog," but "*an* elephant." A primary force in word formation, → inflection, and → composition of Greek.

**EUSEBIAN CANONS.** A set of ten tables devised by Eusebius of Caesarea (ca. A.D. 320) to indicate parallel sections of the four Gospels. He divided the Gospels into numbered sections and placed in parallel columns in the canons the numbers of those sections that contained accounts of the same events. In many → manuscripts, the canons are prefixed and the section numbers, together with references to the canon in which they are listed, are placed in the margin. → Ammonian Sections.

**EUTHALIAN APPARATUS.** A miscellany of introductory notes, summaries, tables of quotations, and lections found in late Greek manuscripts of Paul's letters, Acts, and the → Catholic Epistles. The material was probably revised by Euthalius in the seventh century A.D.

**EXCEPTIVE CLAUSE.** A → clause that depends on another clause and is introduced by "except," "unless"; it makes an exception to something that has preceded. *Heb:* "Do two walk together *unless* they have agreed to do so?" (Amos 3:3). *Gk:* "*unless* your righteousness surpasses that of the Pharisees" (Matt. 5:20). → Conditional Clause.

**EXCLAMATION.** → Interjection.

**EXCURSUS.** A digression that gives an extended discussion of a matter not covered extensively in the main body of the text. Usually placed at the end of the text as an appendix.

**EXECRATION.** A curse; something that is execrated or detested. The word is synonymous with *imprecation.* *Heb:* There are a number of execrations in the OT, e.g., Pss. 83:9–18; 109. *Gk:* Rom. 9:3. → Anathema.

**EXEGESIS.** The use of critical and scholarly procedures to derive the meaning of a passage of Scripture; it is to be distinguished from → exposition and → eisegesis.

**EXEGETE.** The person who does an → exegesis.

**EXEMPLAR.** The → manuscript that serves as the example or standard for a copy of a biblical text.

**EXORDIUM.** The first of seven parts of a classical oration, designed to introduce the subject and catch the hearers' attention; comparable to some Pauline introductions. *Ex:* Gal. 1:6–10. → Proem, → Prologue.

**EXPANDED PARALLELISM.** Another name for → synthetic parallelism.

**EXPANDED TEXT.** → Conflation.

**EXPLANATORY.** Another name for → epexegetical.

**EXPLETIVE.** A word inserted to fill a vacancy in a sentence without adding to the sense (→ impersonal verb and → pleonasm). In English, words such as *there* or *it* occupy the position in word order of subject or object and anticipate a following word or phrase that supplies the meaningful content. *Ex:* "*There* will be earthquakes in various places, and famines" (Mark 13:8).

**EXPLICATIVE.** Another name for → epexegetical.

**EXPLICIT.** Distinctly stated with no disguised or uncertain meaning. → Implicit.

**EXPLICIT QUOTATION.** An OT passage (or extrabiblical source) cited in the NT that shows verbatim agreement with the source and/or is accompanied by an introductory → formula that demonstrates the intention of the author to quote. Also called *citation*.

**EXPOSITION.** A method of elaborating the meaning of a text as determined by → exegesis and showing its contemporary relevance or application without distorting or falsifying its original meaning; it is to be distinguished from → exegesis.

**EXTRABIBLICAL.** Not found in the Bible; also used as another term for → *extracanonical.*

**EXTRACANONICAL.** Extracanonical books are those that were not accepted into the → canon as part of the sacred Scriptures; also called *noncanonical* or *extrabiblical.* → Apocrypha, → Pseudepigrapha.

**FACHPROSA.** German for "technical prose." A recent classification of NT → Koine Greek, attempting to distinguish it from artistic or literary prose.

**FACTITIVE.** A factitive verb expresses an idea of making or rendering something to be of a certain character and hence takes a complement in addition to its object. *Ex:* "But you have made it a 'den of robbers' " (Luke 19:46). → Object Complement.

**FAMILY.** A term used in → textual criticism to describe relationships between extant biblical → manuscripts: a small group of manuscripts, as distinct from a → text-type, that show a marked similarity and likely have a common origin. *Ex:* Family 1 and Family 13 of Greek NT → minuscules.

**FARRAGO.** A confused, frequently ungrammatical construction that is understandable only because of the context. *Heb:* the name Maher-Shalal-Hash-Baz (Isa. 8:3). *Gk:* the nickname Boanerges (Mark 3:17).

**FASCICLE.** A section of a book that is published in installments rather than as a whole.

**FESTSCHRIFT.** A German word used to designate a collection of essays or studies in honor of a well-known scholar, prepared by his colleagues.

**FIGURA ETYMOLOGICA.** Another name for → cognate accusative.

**FIGURATIVE LANGUAGE.** → Figure, Figure of Speech.

**FIGURE, FIGURE OF SPEECH.** The use of words in a way other than the ordinary or literal sense. Figurative language may be expressed by such devices as → metaphor and → simile. *Heb:* "all the trees of the field will clap their hands" (Isa. 55:12). *Gk:* "I am the bread of life" (John 6:35).

**FIN.** Abbreviation of Latin *finis,* "end." Used in a → critical apparatus to refer to the end of a verse or → reading.

**FINAL.** → Telic.

**FINAL CLAUSE.** Another name for a → purpose clause. → Telic.

**FINITE VERB.** From Latin *finio,* "to limit." The finite verb is that part of a verbal construction that limits the subject in terms of → number and → person. In Hebrew, "finite" refers to the → perfect and → imperfect forms of the verb as opposed to the nonfinite forms (→ infinitive, → imperative, and → participle). In Greek, the nonfinite forms are → participle and → infinitive as opposed to the → mood forms.

**FISSION.** In → textual criticism, fission is the dividing up of a single word into two words. *Heb: laḥpōr pērôṯ* in Isa. 2:20 (meaning "to the rodents") according to some scholars should be amended to read *laḥᵃparpārôṯ* ("to the shrew") with the → LXX. → Fusion.

**FL.** Abbreviation of Latin *floruit,* "flourished." Used to indicate the time at which a person or movement flourished. For an illustration, → Apollonian Canon.

**FLORILEGIUM.** Latin for "gathering of flowers." A collection or anthology of written texts; in biblical studies, an anthology of texts from Qumran or in the NT, consisting of messianic → testimonia or → pesher interpretations. *Ex:* the *Florilegium* from Qumran cave four (4QFlor).

**FOLIO.** In a → codex and in printing, a sheet of paper folded once; the size of a book made of sheets folded once; the result is four pages to the sheet. → Quarto, → Octavo.

**FOOT.** The smallest unit in poetry that contains stressed and unstressed syllables.

**FORM.** The shape that a word (→ morpheme) or construction takes in a sentence, as opposed to → function. The form of a word is seen in relation to other words of similar structure (→ morphology).

**FORMAL CORRESPONDENCE.** Another term for → formal equivalence.

**FORMAL EQUIVALENCE.** A type of translation in which the form and structure of the original are reproduced as nearly as possible, in contrast to → dynamic equivalence. Also called *formal correspondence. Ex:* the → NASB stresses formal equivalence, the *Good News Bible* dynamic equivalence, while the *Living Bible* is a → paraphrase.

**FORMAL PARALLELISM.** Another name for → synthetic parallelism.

**FORMATIVE LENGTHENING.** The change of a short vowel to its corresponding long vowel in → vowel gradation.

**FORM CRITICISM.** The analysis of a text according to typical, identifiable forms by which the people of a given cultural context expresses itself linguistically. A good introduction to form criticism is Klaus Koch, *The Growth of the Biblical Tradition.*

**FORMER PROPHETS.** In the Hebrew Bible this is the designation of the books of Joshua, Judges, 1–2 Samuel, and 1–2 Kings.

**FORMGESCHICHTE.** German name for the discipline known as → form criticism.

**FORMULA (pl. FORMULAE, -AS).** A short fixed literary form; especially stereotyped phrases used by NT writers to introduce → explicit quotations of the OT. *Heb:* "This is what the Lord says" is a messenger formula (Jer. 10:1). *Gk:* "As it is written" is an introductory formula (Rom. 2:10).

**FORMULA CRITICISM.** The study of individual words or, usually, groups of words that appear similarly in different passages. These words or groups of words, called → formulae, consistently express the same basic idea, although the contexts in which they appear differ. *Heb:* the messenger formula, "This is what the LORD says" (e.g., Amos 1:3). *Gk:* "I tell you the truth" (John 5:24).

**FORM WORD.** A word with little meaning, often not translated, whose role is largely grammatical—to clarify the meaning and relationships of other words; usually → particles and → conjunctions. Also called a *function word*. *Heb:* the precative *lû*, "if," "oh that!"; the sign of the definite direct object *'ēṯ* (not translated). *Gk:* the → optative *an*.

**FOUR DOCUMENT HYPOTHESIS.** An elaboration of the → two-source hypothesis on the relationship of the → Synoptic Gospels made by B. H. Streeter. He postulated that behind Matthew and Luke lay four sources: → M, the material unique to Matthew (written A.D. 60, Jerusalem); → L, the material unique to Luke (written A.D. 60, Caesarea); Mark (written A.D. 66, Rome), and → Q, the sayings source (written A.D. 50, Antioch).

**FREE FORM.** A type of → morpheme.

**FREQUENTATIVE.** Expresses action that continues throughout a longer or shorter period of time or is repeated occasionally or at fixed intervals. *Heb:* "This went on year after year" (1 Sam. 1:7), lit., "he did year by year." *Gk:* usually expressed by the → imperfect tense; "Now it was the custom at the Feast to release a prisoner" (Mark 15:6). Also called *customary.* → Iterative.

**FRICATIVE.** Frictional rustling of the breath in pronouncing certain consonants (*f, v, s, z*); also called → spirants.

**FRÜHKATHOLIZISMUS.** The German term for → early Catholicism.

**FULCRA.** Latin for "supports." Another name for → matres lectionis.

**FULL VOWELS.** In Hebrew, the vowels that correspond to *a, e, i, o, u.* › Half Vowel.

**FULL WRITING.** Another name for → plena writing.

**FUNCTION.** The work that a word or construction does in a sentence, as opposed to → form. The function of a word is seen in relation to other words in the sentence (→ syntax).

**FUNCTION WORD.** Another name for → form word.

**FUSION.** In → textual criticism, the combining of two separate words into one. *Heb: babbᵉqārîm,* "with oxen," probably stands for an original *babbāqār yām,* "with the oxen the sea" (Amos 6:12 RSV). → Fission.

**FUTURE PERFECT TENSE.** A → tense that expresses action that will be completed before a certain time in the future. *Ex:* He *will have gone* before we arrive. The tense is very rare, even in classical Greek, and is usually formed → periphrastically. There are six periphrastic forms of the tense in the NT (Matt. 16:19; 18:18; Luke 12:52; Heb. 2:13). English translations do not preserve the distinctive force of the future perfect; they usually render it as an emphatic future tense. *Gk:* "whatever you bind on earth *will be bound* in heaven" (Matt. 16:19).

**FUTURE TENSE.** The Greek future → tense is usually a positive assertion about a future activity; it can be predictive, → volitive, or → deliberative and occurs only in the → indicative mood. The Hebrew → *imperfect,* among others, can be the equivalent of a simple future. *Heb:* "I *will put* my law in their minds" (Jer. 31:33). *Gk:* "For sin *shall* not *be* your master" (Rom. 6:14).

**G.** Abbreviation of → Grundlage.

**GATTUNG (pl., GATTUNGEN).** A German word used in → form criticism to refer to the form of a literary entity. The term is being replaced in scholarly circles by → genre.

**GEHENNA.** Greek word derived from the Hebrew "Valley of Hinnom," a ravine south of Jerusalem where human sacrifice was offered during the period of the monarchy. By NT times the word was used in a metaphorical sense as the place of punishment of the wicked dead.

**GEIST.** German for "Spirit."

**GEMARA.** A type of commentary on the → Mishnah produced by the → Amoraim. It contains a variety of proverbs, tales, and customs that relate to rabbinic lore as well as direct expositions of the text. The Mishnah together with the Palestinian Gemara is called the Palestinian or Jerusalem → Talmud; the Mishnah together with the Babylonian Gemara is called the Babylonian Talmud.

**GEMATRIA.** A system of interpretation that looks for the hidden meaning of the Hebrew and Greek text by means of the numerical values of the letters of the alphabet. *Heb:* the numerical equivalent of the literal

Hebrew, "sum of all the sons of Israel" (Num. 1:2) is 603,551, which is almost the exact number of Israelites in the census (Num. 1:46). *Gk:* the number of the beast, 666 (Rev. 13:18), is interpreted by some to refer to Nero.

**GEMINATION.** The lengthening or doubling of a consonant; in Hebrew it is the function of the → *daghesh forte;* in Greek, → liquid consonants are doubled in some instances, but other consonant gemination is due to Semitic influence.

**GENDER.** Gender is distinction as to sex. Hebrew has only two classes of gender, masculine and feminine. When the same form is used to express masculine and feminine, it is called common gender. Greek expresses masculine, feminine, and neuter gender, as does English.

**GENEALOGICAL METHOD.** Establishing the history of the transmission of → manuscripts by working back in time. A task of → textual criticism, defined by Westcott and Hort, that attempts to recover the texts of successive ancestors (manuscripts) by analysis and comparison of their respective descendants. Having established a → text-type, the goal is the recovery of a yet earlier common ancestor. → Stemma Codicum.

**GENEALOGY.** The history of the descent of a person or a family from earlier ancestors. Both the OT and NT contain extensive genealogical lists. *Ex:* 1 Chron. 1:1−9:44; Matt. 1:1−16.

**GENERAL EPISTLES.** Another name for the → Catholic Epistles.

**GENERATIVE GRAMMAR.** A set of formal rules by which the potentially infinite number of sentence structures in a language can be reduced to a finite set. Following the lead of Noam Chomsky, the most influential type of generative theory features rules for transforming one sentence into another; such grammars are usually called "transformational generative" (TG).

**GENERIC.** A term used in grammatical analysis to express classes or groups. It is a common use of the Greek article, e.g., "*the* poor in spirit" (Matt. 5:3).

**GENITIVE.** The → case that expresses possession or specifies a relationship that can be expressed in English by "of." In Hebrew this is called a → construct relationship. The Greek genitive is the specifying case answering the question "What kind?" *Heb:* "the expanse *of the sky*" (Gen. 1:21). *Gk:* "a baptism *of repentance* for the forgiveness *of sins*" (Mark 1:4).

**GENITIVE ABSOLUTE.** In Greek, an → absolute phrase composed of a → participle and → substantive (in most cases), both in the → genitive case. It functions as an adverbial clause with the substantive the subject of the action. *Gk:* "While Gallio was proconsul of Achaia" (Acts 18:12).

**GENIZA, GENIZAH.** A room attached to a synagogue where documents no longer in use were stored or hidden. *Ex:* the Cairo Genizah discovered in 1896.

**GENRE.** As applied to literature this term denotes a distinctive group (or a structural scheme) with respect to style, form, purpose, etc. Now being used in → form criticism to replace the term → Gattung.

**GENTILIC.** A classification of nouns that denotes various individuals belonging to the same class; also called *ethnica*. In Hebrew, these nouns are recognized by special gentilic endings. *Heb:* Israelite, Moabite, etc. are written with gentilic endings. *Gk:* a variety of stem → suffixes are used, but the Hebrew gentilic appears in Greek -*itēs*, e.g., Rom. 11:1. → Patronymic.

**GERUND, GERUNDIVE.** A verbal noun form that in English ends in -*ing* and is used like a noun. It is sometimes called a *participial noun*. It may take an object or be modified by an adjective or adverb. *Ex: Eating* is allowed in this room; *running* is good exercise.

**GESCHICHTE.** A German term for "history". → Historie.

**GEZERAH SAWAH.** The second of Hillel's seven → middot, the analogy of identical words. The exegetical principle, easily abused, that identical words occurring in different places in Scripture have a common interpretation. *Heb:* "counted" in Gen. 15:6 (NIV, "credited") and Ps. 32:2. *Gk:* the same passages employed by Paul in Rom. 4:3, 8.

**GLOBAL AORIST.** Another name for → constative aorist.

**GLOSS.** A word or words added to explain the text. It is believed that glosses were frequently transferred from the margin into the text itself, either accidentally or intentionally. *Heb:* some scholars say that the word "Israel" in Isa. 49:3 is a gloss that was added to identify the servant as the people Israel. *Gk:* Luther's famous gloss on Rom. 3:28 yields the reading "justified by faith *alone.*"

**GLOSSATOR.** A person who makes → glosses in biblical texts.

**GLOSSOLALIA.** The gift of speaking in tongues. → Charisma.

**GLOTTAL STOP.** A momentary closing of the air passage before the pronunciation of a vowel or between the pronunciation of two vowels.

**GNOMIC.** In grammatical analysis, an aspect of the verb that indicates a timeless truth, → *maxim,* or proverbial saying. *Heb:* "If two lie down together, they will keep warm" (Eccl. 4:11); *Gk:* "The grass withers and the flowers fall" (1 Peter 1:24; cf. Isa. 40:7).

**GNOSIS/GNOSTIC/GNOSTICISM.** From Greek *gnosis,* "knowledge." A widespread and highly diverse religious movement with roots in Greek philosophy and folk religion. Its chief emphases are the utter transcendence of God, created matter as fallen and evil, and salvation by esoteric knowledge. The Gnostic heresy or Gnosticism is the developed system that emerged in the second century A.D. and is associated with the names of Marcion, Basilides, and Valentinius. Sources of information on Gnosticism are the church fathers—Tertullian, Irenaeus, Hippolytus, and Origen—and the Gnostic texts of → Nag Hammadi. By convention some scholars refer to pre-Christian evidence as gnosis, reserving the term Gnosticism for the later heresy; other scholars prefer the terms *incipient* or *proto-Gnosticism* for pre-Christian and NT evidences.

**GORGIAN FIGURES.** Rhetorical figures developed by Gorgias of Sicily (485–375 B.C.), the originator of artistic Greek prose; literary arrangement of words and phrases using → parallelism and → assonance. → Paronomasia.

**GOSPEL CRITICISM.** Gospel criticism is a branch of → biblical criticism; it includes such things as → textual criticism, → source criticism, → historical criticism, → form criticism, and → redaction criticism as applied to the → Gospels.

**GOSPELS.** The first four books of the NT.

**GOY (pl., GOYIM).** Hebrew word for "nation," "people," or "Gentiles."

**GRAMMATICO-HISTORICAL CRITICISM.** This discipline makes use of many critical disciplines in order to shed light on the Scriptures and to understand them better. It studies the historical background together with grammatical, syntactical, and linguistic factors. It usually combines exegesis with exposition and is used largely in conservative circles.

**GRIESBACH HYPOTHESIS.** A solution to the → Synoptic problem proposed by J. J. Griesbach (1783), which holds that Matthew was the earliest Gospel, that Luke depended on Matthew, and that Mark later used the two, producing an abbreviated and conflated version (→ conflation). Chief among contemporary advocates is W. R. Farmer; also called the two-gospel hypothesis.

**GRIMM'S LAW.** Rules governing the change of consonants in Indo-European language, especially in → cognate words. *Ex:* Greek *p* becomes *v* or *f,* as in Greek *patēr,* German *Vater,* and English *father.*

**GRUNDLAGE.** German term for foundational tradition, an underlying oral source; a hypothetical common tradition behind the → J and → E documents. Also referred to as G.

**GRUNDSCHRIFT.** Same as → Grundlage, except that it is a written source.

**GUTTURALS.** The → mute consonants whose sounds are produced when the front of the tongue approaches the palate of the mouth. Four letters in Hebrew, *aleph, he, heth,* and *ayin,* are the guttural letters (*resh* has some guttural characteristics). Hebrew gutturals cannot be doubled, prefer *a*-class vowels, and → composite *shewas.* In Greek, the guttural letters are *gamma, kappa,* and *chi;* also called *velars, laryngeals,* or *palatals.*

# *H*

**HABER (pl., HABERIM).** Hebrew for "associate," a comrade in a fraternity (called a *haburah*) of Pharisees; a religious devotee who dutifully followed rabbinic prescriptions, in contrast to the → *am ha'arets.*

**HABIRU.** A group of people found all over the ancient Near East during the second millennium B.C. Their exact identity is disputed. They appear in historical records as nomads, soldiers, slaves, merchants, and outlaws. Some scholars have tried to equate them with the Hebrews.

**HAFTARAH, HAPHTORAH.** Designated passages of Scriptures to be read in the course of the year in the synagogue. The passages are chosen from the → Torah and from the → Prophets. → Parash.

**HAGGADAH/HAGGADIC.** The nonlegal sections of rabbinic literature, featuring imaginative exposition and explanatory narration of OT texts, enhanced by anecdotes and spiritual maxims. → Halakah, → Midrash.

**HAGIOGRAPHA.** Another name for the third division of the Hebrew Bible. Also called the *Writings* or the *Ketubim.* They include the Psalms, Proverbs, Job, Song of Solomon, Ruth, Lamentations, Ecclesiastes, Esther, Daniel, Ezra, Nehemiah, 1–2 Chronicles. → Torah, → Nebiim.

**ḤAKHAMIM.** Hebrew, "sages" or "wise men." Interpreters of the Jewish oral law who came from the upper strata of society and did their work without receiving compensation. They originally functioned as officers of rabbinic courts in Palestine and Babylonia.

**HALAKAH/HALAKIC.** The Jewish oral laws of the → Tannaim that supplemented or explained the laws of the OT; the legal portions of rabbinic literature as distinct from → haggadah, emphasizing rules for conduct of life. These normative interpretations are preserved in various → midrashim, the → Mishnah, and the → Talmud.

**HALF VOWEL.** In the Hebrew language, another name for the simple → *shewa* and the → composite (or compound) *shewa*. The simple *shewa* is written under the consonant to which it is related. → Semivowel.

**HALLEL.** From Hebrew for "praise." A song of praise to the Lord. Psalms 113–18 are sometimes called the *Egyptian Hallel*. Psalms 120–136 are sometimes called the *Great Hallel* (although they are more frequently called *Songs of Ascents, Songs of Degrees,* or *Pilgrimage Songs*).

**HANUKKAH, CHANUKKAH.** A Jewish religious festival, the Feast of Dedication or Feast of Lights, that is observed in Judaism in the month of December. It finds its historical origin in the cleansing of the temple by Judas Maccabeus in 164 B.C. from the pollution of pagan worship.

**HAPAX LEGOMENON (pl., HAPAX LEGOMENA).** The single occurrence of a word in a selected body of literature, especially the single occurrence of a Hebrew word in the OT or of a Greek word in the NT. *Heb: b$^e$ʻāthāh,* "terror" (Jer. 8:15). *Gk: allotriepiskopos,* "mischief-maker," "meddler" (1 Peter 4:15).

**HAPHTORAH.** → Haftarah.

**HAPLOGRAPHY.** The accidental omission of a letter, letter group, or word(s) that should have been written twice; it is the opposite of → dittography. *Ex: partive* instead of *partitive.*

**HARMONY OF THE GOSPELS.** A rearrangement of the four Gospels on a chronological basis so that they present a unified, continuous life and ministry of Jesus; the earliest known example is Tatian's → Diatessaron. *Ex:* A. T. Robertson, *A Harmony of the Gospels for Students of the Life of Christ.* → Synopsis of the Gospels.

**HAUSTAFELN.** The German term for → household codes.

**HEBRAISM.** A word or idiom derived from the Hebrew language; in biblical studies it refers especially to any part of the → Septuagint or NT Greek that shows the influence of Hebrew style and terminology.

**HEIGHTENING.** In Hebrew, the change of a short vowel to a long vowel. → Tone-long Vowel.

**HEILSGESCHICHTE.** A German word translated variously as "salvation history," "redemptive history," or "sacred history"; it interprets the Bible as the ongoing story of God's redemptive activity in history.

**HELLENISTIC AGE.** The era of cultural unity in the Greek East brought about by the conquests of Alexander the Great. The period extends from the death of Alexander (323 B.C.) to the rise of the Augustan principate (31 B.C.).

**HELLENIZE/HELLENIZATION.** The adoption or imposition of Greek language and culture; a tendency accelerated in Judaism during the → Hellenistic age.

**HEMISTICH.** A half-line of poetry; the term is sometimes used to describe the complete line. → Stich.

**HENDIADYS.** In the biblical languages, the expression of a single idea by two nouns or verbs, usually connected by "and." *Heb:* "Let them serve as signs *to* mark seasons" (Gen. 1:14), lit., "for signs *and* for seasons"; "may all . . . be turned back *in* disgrace" (Ps. 40:14), lit., "turn back *and* be disgraced". *Gk:* "my hope *in* the resurrection of the dead" (Acts 23:6), lit., "hope *and* resurrection."

**HENOTHEISM.** Belief in one god, though not denying the existence of other gods.

**HEPTATEUCH.** The first seven books of the OT.

**HEREM.** A Hebrew word meaning "ban" or "accursed." The divine sanction of the destruction of the enemy, his family, and property in the → holy war. *Ex:* Samuel's orders to Saul to "totally destroy" the Amalekites (1 Sam. 15:3).

**HERMENEUTICS.** Principles of interpretation; correctly understanding the thought of an author and communicating that thought to others. → Exegesis, → Middot.

**HERMETIC LITERATURE.** Popular Greek theosophical writings of the first three centuries A.D., ascribed to Hermes Trismegistus, "thrice-great Hermes," a designation of the Egyptian god Thoth. An amalgam of Egyptian religion and Greek → dualism cast in the literary form of Platonic dialogues. The primary collection of eighteen treatises is called *Corpus Hermeticum,* the first and most important being *Poimandres;* like the other treatises it is → syncretistic and → Gnostic in outlook.

**HESED.** A Hebrew word translated as "mercy," "loyalty," "covenant love," etc. Because it has such a wide range of meaning, some commentaries use the Hebrew word instead of an English translation. It is also spelled *chesed* (following a different transliteration system).

**HESYCHIAN TEXT.** Another name for the → Alexandrian text.

**HETEROCLISIS.** In Greek, the irregular → inflection of a noun; a word that alternates between → declensions and/or → genders. *Gk: zēlos,* "zeal," alternates between second declension masculine and third declension neuter. → Metaplasm.

**HETERONYM.** Words that are spelled the same but are pronounced differently (e.g., *lead, lead*). This phenomenon is not characteristic of Hebrew. Greek exhibits several accented forms such as *ménei,* "he abides," and *meneî,* "he will abide."

**HEXAEMERON.** The creation of the world in six days as found in Genesis 1.

**HEXAPLA.** An edition of the OT in six parallel columns, prepared by Origen. The columns are: the Hebrew text, the Hebrew text transliterated into Greek script, → Aquila, → Symmachus, the → Septuagint, and → Theodotion. In some parts of the OT, especially the Psalms, further columns were added, containing anonymous Greek versions; these are called the *Quinta, Sexta,* and *Septima,* the "fifth," "sixth," and "seventh" Greek versions. The Hexapla is extant only in fragments.

**HEXAPLARIC.** A word used to describe → manuscripts that contain, in whole or part, the additions by Origen in the fifth column of the → *Hexapla.*

**HEXATEUCH.** The first six books of the OT.

**HIATUS.** The succession of vowels in the final and initial sounds of adjoining words; the resulting break in speech is unpleasing and was avoided in classical prose. The only NT book that studiously avoids hiatus is Hebrews.

**HIERATIC.** A → cursive script, derived from Egyptian → hieroglyphs, written from right to left and developed for speed of writing on → papyrus.

**HIEROCRACY.** The form of government in which priests and religious leaders exercise authority; it was characteristic of Judah in the postexilic period.

**HIEROGLYPH/HIEROGLYPHIC.** A kind of picture writing used by the ancient Egyptians.

**HIEROGRAPH.** A sacred symbol.

**HIEROS LOGOS.** A term for what is told about an event and/or its location as explanation of its sacred origin and significance. *Ex:* Gen. 28:1–17 is a hieros logos concerning the Bethel sanctuary.

**HIFIL.** → Hiphil.

**HIGHER CRITICISM.** A type of biblical criticism that deals with matters such as historical background, authorship, date of writing, etc., as opposed to lower or → textual criticism.

**HIPHIL, HIFIL.** A verbal form in Hebrew that expresses → causative action and active → voice. *Heb:* "So God made the expanse and separated [lit., caused separation] the water" (Gen. 1:7).

**HIREQ COMPAGINIS.** → Compaginis Letters.

**HISTORICAL CRITICISM.** A term that is used loosely to describe all the methodologies related to → biblical criticism. It was developed especially in the nineteenth century when it was believed that reality was uniform and universal and could be discovered by human reason and investigations. Also, it is used to mean the historical setting of a document (such as time, place, sources, etc.). The term is also used to describe an emphasis on historical, philological, and archaeological analysis of the biblical texts.

**HISTORICAL PRESENT.** In both Hebrew and Greek, a → present tense used in → narrative to report action that occurred in the past for a vivid portrayal of historical scenes. The present force is usually lost in translation. *Gk:* "A man with leprosy *came* [lit., comes] to him" (Mark 1:40).

**HISTORIE.** A German term used in contemporary criticism to denote that which is public and verifiable according to the methods of historiography. Its counterpart, *Geschichte*, refers to the significance of historical facts for faith, which is not open in the same way to historical scrutiny. → Heilsgeschichte.

**HISTORY OF RELIGIONS SCHOOL.** An early-twentieth-century German school of interpretation that applied the principles of → comparative religion to the study of early Christianity. It held that, as a religion of the Roman empire, Christianity was a → syncretistic faith borrowing from → mystery religions and → Gnosticism. Chief proponents of this school were R. Reitzenstein (1861–1931) and W. Bousset (1865–1920). Also called → *religio-historical criticism.*

**HITHPAEL.** A verbal form in Hebrew that expresses intensive or emphatic action (classified by some grammars as → causative action) and → reflexive → voice. For this emphasis in Greek, → middle voice. *Heb:* "A group of adventurers gathered around [lit., gathered themselves around] him" (Judg. 11:3).

**ḤOKMAH.** The Hebrew word for → wisdom. Some commentaries use the Hebrew word instead of the English translation.

**HOLINESS CODE.** A term coined by A. Klostermann in 1877 to refer to Leviticus 17–26.

**HOLLOW VERB.** In Hebrew, a biconsonantal → root that has a long vowel between the two root consonants. These are the *ayin yod* and *ayin waw* verbs. *Heb:* šûḇ, śîm.

**HOLY WAR.** A term used by OT scholars to describe the wars of conquest of the Israelites at the time of their entrance into Canaan. → Ḥerem.

**HOMILY.** An admonitory discourse or sermon; a Jewish sermonic form current in synagogue worship during the NT period: a freely structured discourse with biblical quotations and keywords. Extant in Palestinian → midrashim of the → yelammedenu type, in → Hellenistic forms like 4 Maccabees, and in the NT letters of Hebrews and James. *Gk:* "a word of exhortation" (Heb. 13:22).

**HOMOGENEOUS.** Consonants or vowels whose sound is of the same nature so that under certain conditions they may readily merge; in Greek it mainly occurs in → vowel contraction. *Heb: ʿāśû* for ʿāśûn (Job 41:25). *Gk: edeito* for *edeeto* (Luke 8:38). → Syncope.

**HOMOGRAPH.** A word that is spelled similarly to another word but has a different meaning. *Heb: rāʿāh,* "evil," *rāʿāh,* "to feed," *rēʿeh,* "friend." *Gk: tróchos,* "course," *trochós,* "wheel." → Heteronym. → Homonym.

**HOMOIOARCHTON.** The same error as → homoioteleuton but caused by similar or identical *beginnings* of words close together; less frequent than homoioteleuton.

**HOMOIOSIS.** The repetition of the same or similar letters or words in a text that results in errors in copying. Examples are → haplography and → homoioteleuton.

**HOMOIOTELEUTON.** An error, usually of omission, made in copying a text when two words stand close together and have similar or identical *endings;* the copyist skips from the first of these words to the second and so omits several words. → Homoioarchton.

**HOMOLOGIA.** A Greek term for → confessional formula.

**HOMOLOGOUMENA.** Books of the Bible that were received by all alike, i.e., undisputed books of the NT → canon (see Eusebius, *Ecclesiastical History* 3.25). → Antilegomena.

**HOMONYM.** A word that is pronounced like another but is different in meaning. *Ex: piece, peace. Heb: lō', "no," lô, "to him"; ḥāṣēr, "enclosure," ḥāṣēr, "village." Gk: tis, "someone," tís, "who?"; lusō, "I will release," lusō, "I might release".* → Homograph.

**HOMOPHONE.** Two different characters with the same phonetic value. *Ex: site, cite; Heb: śin, samek.*

**HOMOPHONY.** In → textual criticism, the substitution of one → homonym for another. *Heb: lô, "to him," substituted for lō', "not." Gk: tís, "who?" for tis, "someone."*

**HOMORGANIC.** Consonants that are produced by the same organ of speech. *Heb: gimel* and *kaph. Gk: beta* and *pi.*

**HOPHAL.** A verbal form in Hebrew that expresses → causative action and → passive → voice. *Heb:* "Let seven of his male descendants *be given* [hophal] to us" (2 Sam. 21:6).

**HORTATORY.** → Cohortative.

**HOUSEHOLD CODES.** NT → paraenesis concerning domestic relationships: husbands and wives, parents and children, and masters and slaves. The codes, which are similar in form, are based on the principle of reciprocity and mutual submission in Christ. Literary and ethical parallels are found in first-century Stoicism. *Gk:* Eph. 5:22–6:9; Col. 3:18–4:1; and 1 Peter 2:18–3:7.

**HYMN.** In → form criticism, a term used to designate a song of praise of God. *Heb: Pss.* 8, 100, 103, 113. *Gk:* Luke 1–2; Phil. 2:5–11; 1 Tim. 3:16.

**HYPERBATON.** The artificial displacement of a word or phrase from its natural sequence; a device for emphasis, if indeed the flexible → word order of Hebrew and Greek can be said to have a natural sequence.

**HYPERBOLE.** An exaggeration for the purpose of emphasis and without any intention of deception. *Heb:* "David [has slain] his tens of thousands" (1 Sam. 18:7). *Gk:* "from this one man . . . came descendants as numerous as the stars in the sky and as countless as the sand on the seashore" (Heb. 11:12).

**HYPOCORISTICON, HYPOCORISM.** The shortening of a name by abbreviation, or the affixing of a → diminutive ending; a nickname. *Heb:* Coniah (Jer. 22:24) for Jeconiah (Jer. 24:1). *Gk:* Silas (Acts 15:22) for Silvanus (1 Thess. 1:1).

**HYPONEMA (pl., HYPONEMATA).** Greek for "commentary." A series of notes on an ancient text as distinct from a → scholion; in classical antiquity invariably published in continuous form as a separate → manuscript.

**HYPOTAXIS.** Grammatical → subordination; highly developed in the clause structure of literary Greek in contrast to the → parataxis or coordination of sentences in Hebrew. *Gk:* use of subordinating → conjunction and adverbial → participles in → Koine.

**HYPOTHESIS.** A conjectural explanation that has not yet been verified but leads to scientific understanding; a preliminary step towards a theory, which is more comprehensive and better grounded.

**HYSTERON PROTERON.** Greek for the "latter (comes before the) former." A figurative device related to → anastrophe in which the temporal order of events is reversed by an inversion of phrases or clauses. *Ex:* Ps. 9:15–16; the antecedent principle, the Lord being "known by his justice" (v. 16), follows the evidence of its outworking among the "nations" ensnared by their own devices (v. 15).

# I

**ICTUS.** A stressed or accented syllable.

**IDEOGRAM.** Progression in writing beyond → pictogram. It expresses some idea associated with the thing shown in the picture.

**IDIOM.** An expression used in a language that is peculiar or unique to that language in grammatical construction or meaning. Hebrew and Greek are replete with idiomatit expressions. *Ex:* "As the Lord lives," "son of the bridal chamber."

**ILLATIVE.** Another name for → inferential.

**IMAGERY.** Another designation for → figurative language. → Figure, Figure of Speech.

**IMAGO DEI.** Latin for "image of God" (Gen. 1:27).

**IMITATIO CHRISTI.** Latin for "imitation of Christ." The act of discipleship, taking one's cross and following Christ, even to death. In criticism, a literary convention for passages that emphasize this theme. *Ex:* Matt. 10:37–39; 1 Peter 2:21.

**IMPERATIVE.** A verb or verbal → mood that expresses command or makes a request. *Heb:* "*Give* us water to drink" (Exod. 17:2). *Gk:* "*Give* us each day our daily bread" (Luke 11:3).

**IMPERFECT.** In Hebrew, the form of the verb used to express action that is incomplete or unfinished. *Heb:* "What if they do not believe me" (Exod. 4:1). The Greek imperfect → tense expresses incomplete, → linear action in past time. *Gk:* "People *were eating* and *drinking . . .*" (Luke 17:28). Other regular uses of the tense include → iterative, → frequentative, → inceptive, and → conative.

**IMPERSONAL VERB.** A verb denoting the action of an unspecified agent and thus expressing no personal subject. *Heb: wayᵉhî,* "and it came to pass." *Gk: dei,* "it is necessary." Noted in translation by → expletive *it* or *there.*

**IMPLICIT.** Information that is not actually stated but is understood or assumed. The sovereignty of God over all peoples is implicit in messages of judgment against the nations (Jer. 46–51; Rev. 20:11–15). It is the opposite of → explicit.

**IMPRECATION.** → Execration.

**IMPROPER DIPHTHONG.** In Greek, the → diphthong that is formed by the writing of → *iota* subscript. Also, diphthongs *ei* and *ou* formed by vowel contraction are sometimes called *spurious diphthongs.*

**IN., INIT.** Abbreviations of Latin *initium,* "beginning." Used in a → critical apparatus to refer to the beginning of a verse or reading. → Fin.

**INCEPTIVE ACTION.** Represents action as beginning to take place. *Heb:* "May the day of my birth perish" (Job 3:3), i.e., from the moment the birth process began. *Gk:* "He *began to teach* them" (inceptive imperfect; Mark 2:13). Also called *incipient, inchoative,* or *ingressive.*

**INCHOATIVE.** Another term for → inceptive.

**INCIPIENT.** Another term for → inceptive.

**INCIPIT.** Latin for "[here] begins." The name of a fixed phrase that introduces a daily reading from a Gospel → lectionary. *Ex:* "The Lord said to his disciples."

**INCLUSIO.** Poetic device whereby the opening word or theme reappears at the end. The first word may include the overall meaning of a number of words that follow it, or the first concept in a series of poetic concepts or units is restated in the final unit. *Heb:* '*ārîḇ* in Jer. 2:9; Eccl. 1:2; Song of Sol. 1:2b–3a. *Gk: agapē* in 1 Cor. 13:4; Rom. 8:35–39.

**INDEFINITE PLURAL.** The use of an indefinite subject, "they," where the context does not admit a specific agent (→ impersonal verb); translated in sense as a passive construction; a → Semitism, especially in the Gospels. *Heb:* "let a place be assigned to me" (1 Sam. 27:5), lit., "let *them* assign me a place". *Gk:* "your life will be demanded from you" (Luke 12:20), lit., "*they* are demanding your life from you."

**INDEPENDENT CLAUSE.** Another name for → main clause.

**INDETERMINATE.** Indefinite; the opposite of → determinate.

**INDICATIVE MOOD.** A verb → mood of definite assertion that states a fact or asks a question. *Gk:* "There *is* rejoicing in the presence of the angels of God" (Luke 15:10).

**INDIRECT DISCOURSE.** The words of a speaker reported indirectly in narrative discourse, usually by a rephrased construction introduced by *that. Heb:* "For I told him *that* I would judge his family forever" (1 Sam. 3:13). *Gk:* "He has told us *that* you always have pleasant memories" (1 Thess. 3:6). Also called *oratio obliqua.* → Direct Discourse.

**INDIRECT OBJECT.** The person or thing indirectly affected by the action of the verb, i.e., the secondary goal of the verb's action. *Heb:* "First sell *me* your birthright" (Gen. 25:31). *Gk:* "Father, give *me* my share of the estate" (Luke 15:12). → Dative Case.

**INDUCTIVE METHOD.** → Deductive Method.

**INERRANCY/INERRANT.** The doctrine that the Bible is free from error or mistake; its rationale usually is based on → verbal inspiration and is restricted to the → autographs, which would be free from textual corruption. The term *infallibility* properly means the Bible is incapable of error, not liable to deceive or mislead. Although the adjectives *inerrant* and *infallible* are often used synonymously, some scholars apply the word *infallible* only to what the Bible teaches, in order to avoid the connotation of historical and scientific accuracy in all matters implied in the word *inerrant.*

**INFALLIBILITY/INFALLIBLE.** → Inerrancy.

**INFERENTIAL.** A particle or conjunction that introduces an inference or deduction from a previous statement; in Hebrew, *kî* and *'ašer;* in Greek, *ara, gar,* and *oun.* Sometimes also called *illative* or substituted for → causal. *Heb:* "Wail, O pine tree, *for* the cedar tree has fallen" (Zech. 11:2). *Gk:* "*Therefore,* since we have been justified through faith" (Rom. 5:1).

**INFINITIVE.** A → verbal noun that has characteristics of both verbs and nouns. In English usually introduced by *to.* Hebrew has both infinitive absolute and infinitive construct forms. *Heb:* "I am the Lord, who brought you out of Ur of the Chaldeans *to give* you this land" (Gen. 15:7). The Greek infinitive is used as a → substantive, in → subordinate clauses, with → prepositions, and in → epexegesis. *Gk:* "For to me, *to live* is Christ and *to die* is gain" (Phil. 1:21).

**INFINITIVE ABSOLUTE.** A form of the Hebrew infinitive that may function in a number of ways: to express certainty or intensification ("you will *surely* die," Gen. 2:17); to express repeated or continued action ("Be *ever* hearing," Isa. 6:9); as a finite verb ("They . . . *broke* the jars," Judg. 7:19); to express an emphatic imperative (*"Remember* the Sabbath day," Exod. 20:8).

**INFIX.** An → affix inserted within a → root or → stem instead of at the beginning (→ prefix) or at the end (→ suffix). A characteristic of Semitic languages, where forms of the verb are indicated by infixes in the consonantal root, but not applicable to Greek. *Heb:* → energic *nun* in Ps. 50:23; the → *daghesh forte* in the middle consonant of the → intensive stems.

**INFLECTION.** The addition of → affixes to a → stem in order to modify its meaning; a collective term used to describe all grammatical changes that indicate → case, → gender, → number, → tense, → person, → voice, → mood, etc. Greek is a highly inflected language, Hebrew is not.

**INGRESSIVE.** → Inceptive.

**INIT.** → In.

**INSCRIPTION.** Engraved writing on durable materials such as stone, wood, or metal; the term includes graffiti but usually excludes coins (→ numismatics), → papyrus, and → parchment.

**INSTRUMENTAL CASE.** A noun → case that expresses agency or means; it is also called *casus instrumentalis.* In Hebrew it is frequently expressed by *beth,* "with," prefixed to the word. *Heb:* "He will cut down the forest thickets *with an ax"* (Isa. 10:34). *Gk:* "For it is *by* grace you have been saved" (Eph. 2:8).

**INTENSIVE STEM.** A verbal form in Hebrew that intensifies or emphasizes the action of the verb. The three principal intensive → stems are → piel, → pual, and → hithpael.

**INTENTIONAL FALLACY.** The error of studying a literary work in order to establish or assess the author's intention rather than concentrating on what the text actually says. Modern → literary criticism tends to the view that a text's meaning is detached from the author's intention and control, hence literary–critical insights must be deliberately ahistorical.

**INTER ALIA.** Latin for "among other things."

**INTERJECTION.** That which is interjected; a word or words that express an element of surprise; also called *exclamation*. Interjection may be expressed in Hebrew or Greek by certain interjectory words (e.g., Hush! Woe! Behold!) or by the context; it usually does not have a grammatical connection with the rest of the sentence.

**INTERLINEAR BIBLE.** A Bible that contains an English translation written between the lines of the biblical text printed in Hebrew or Greek.

**INTERNAL OBJECT.** Another name for → cognate accusative.

**INTERPOLATION.** A later insertion of material into the text.

**INTERROGATIVE PARTICLE.** A word that introduces a question. *Heb:* among the more common interrogative particles are *mî*, "who?" *māh* "what?" *Gk:* common interrogatives are *tis*, "who?" *pōs* "how?"

**INTERTESTAMENTAL PERIOD.** The period between the completion of the writing of the OT Scriptures and the beginning of the NT era.

**INTERVOCALIC.** A term used in → phonetics to refer to a consonant sound used between two vowels, often producing a greater → voiced sound.

**INTRANSITIVE.** An intransitive verb is one that does not

have a receiver of the action. *Ex:* "I did not *run* or *labor* for nothing" (Phil. 2:16). → Transitive.

**INTROVERTED PARALLELISM.** Another name for → chiasmus.

**INVECTIVE.** A violent denunciation or accusation; some OT and NT invectives are introduced by the word "Woe." *Heb:* "Woe to you who are complacent in Zion" (Amos 6:1). *Gk:* "Woe to you, Korazin!" (Matt. 11:21).

**INVERTED NUN.** The reversal of a *nun* in the Hebrew text to prevent its being considered part of the text; its significance is disputed. There are nine occurrences in the OT, e.g., before Num. 10:35. See Ernest Würthwein, *The Text of the Old Testament,* p. 13, for a list of all occurrences.

**INVERTED PARALLELISM.** Another name for → chiasmus.

**IOTACISM.** Another name for → *itacism.*

**IOTA SUBSCRIPT/IOTA ADSCRIPT.** When Greek *iota* follows long *alpha, eta,* or *omega* in a → diphthong, it is written below (subscript) the first vowel and not pronounced. In Greek manuscripts until the twelfth century A.D., *iota,* if written, appeared on the line (adscript) but was not pronounced; it is also adscript in → uncial writing. *Gk: anthrōpǭ, anthrōpōi.*

**IPSISSIMA VERBA/IPSISSIMA VOX.** Latin, "the very words"/"the very voice." The exact words or language spoken or written by an individual and preserved without any change. Especially applied to the actual words of Jesus as preserved in the Gospels as distinct from sayings attributed to Him by the early church; if the actual words are not preserved, one seeks the actual message or "the very voice."

**IRONY.** A kind of humor, ridicule, or sarcasm in which the true meaning intended is the opposite of the literal sense of the words. *Heb:* "Woe to those who are heroes at drinking wine and champions at mixing drinks" (Isa. 5:22). *Gk:* "I am not in the least inferior to the 'super-apostles'" (2 Cor. 12:11); "We are fools for Christ, but you are so wise in Christ!" (1 Cor. 4:10).

**ISAGOGICS.** Literally, "a leading into." Introductory study preliminary to actual → exegesis and concern with the literary history and text of the Bible.

**ISOCOLON.** A → colon of equal length with another; especially successive members of a poetic or prose unit.

**ITACISM.** The blending of Greek → vowels and → diphthongs during the NT era into the *i* sound, thus the accidental confusion in NT manuscripts of seven vowels or diphthongs that had a similar pronunciation. *Gk: ei, i, ē, ē* (subscript), *u, ui,* and *oi.* Also called *iotacism.*

**ITALA.** Another name for → Old Latin.

**ITERATIVE.** Action of the verb depicted as repeated or as an interrupted activity, continuing at intervals; often used as the equivalent of → frequentative or customary, though some restrict the latter to habitual activity done from time to time, e.g., "he used to go." *Gk:* "She *kept this up* for many days" (Acts 16:18).

**ITTURE SOPHERIM.** Certain words that were omitted by the → scribes; the majority of these are indicated in the → Masora of → BHS. See also Ernst Würthwein, *The Text of the Old Testament,* p. 15.

*J*

**J.** Abbreviation of Jahwist (→ *Yahwist*). → JEDP.

**JAHWEH.** → Yahweh.

**JAHWIST.** → Yahwist.

**JB.** Abbreviation for the *Jerusalem Bible*, a translation by French scholars published in 1961; published in English in 1966.

**JEDP.** Terminology used in the → documentary hypothesis to designate the documents identified by this method of analysis: J = Jahwist, dated ca. 950 B.C., E = Elohist, dated ca. 850 B.C.; D = Deuteronomist, dated ca. 622 B.C.; P = Priestly, dated ca. 500–450 B.C. Proponents of this theory believe that J and E were combined ca. 750 B.C., to which D was added ca. 620 B.C., with P added in the postexilic period, giving the → Pentateuch its final form as we know it by 400 B.C. This hypothesis was given its classical expression by Julius Wellhausen in 1878. → Source Criticism.

**JEHOVAH.** A pronunciation of → Yahweh that began in medieval times out of a misunderstanding of the vowels of the name Adonai (Lord) written with the consonants JHVH by the → Masoretes. This combination of vowels and consonants produces the hybrid "Jehovah" in English. However, the vowels were intended to instruct the reader to substitute the name Adonai for the sacred unpronounceable name.

**JERUSALEM TALMUD.** → Gemara.

**JEWISH PUBLICATION SOCIETY BIBLE.** A translation of the OT by Jewish scholars. Published as *The Torah* (1962, 2nd ed., 1982), *The Prophets* (1978), and *The Writings* (1982).

**JOHANNINE COMMA.** An → interpolation in the text of 1 John 5:7–8, found in the → textus receptus and late → manuscripts of the Vulgate: ". . . in heaven: the Father, the Word, and the Holy Spirit, and these three are one. And there are three that testify on earth: . . ." (see the NIV footnote). It probably originated as a marginal → gloss in the → Old Latin versions of the fifth century A.D.

**JUDAIZER/JUDAIZE.** A collective term for the opponents of Paul who insisted upon observance of the law and ritual circumcision for Gentile converts. The verb means "to live like a Jew," "to conform to Judaism" when used → intransitively, "to bring into conformity with Judaism" when used → transitively. *Gk:* "you force Gentiles *to follow Jewish customs*" (Gal. 2:14).

**JUSSIVE.** → Modal → aspect of the verb with the same function as the → cohortative, but ordinarily it appears in the second or third person in Hebrew. The Greek jussive in the second or third person was little used, being replaced by the → imperative. *Heb:* "And God said, 'Let there be light'" (Gen. 1:3). → Volitive.

**KAIGE RECENSION.** An early revision of the → Septuagint; the name comes from the peculiar translation of the Hebrew particle *gam* ("also") by Greek *kaige;* another name for the → recension is *Proto-Theodotion.*

**KAIROS/KAIROTIC.** A term derived from Greek that describes a period of time that has special significance, cf. nodal points in → Heilsgeschichte. The Exodus was a kairotic event for the ancient Israelites; the incarnation was a kairotic event for Christians.

**KAL.** Variant spelling of → Qal.

**KAPH VERITATIS.** A belief that the letter *kaph,* used as an inseparable preposition ("like/as") in Hebrew, is sometimes used → pleonastically, i.e., it is used not to introduce similarity but simply to introduce the → predicate.

**KEMNEFAṢ LETTERS.** A → mnemonic device containing the Hebrew letters that have alternate final forms: *kaph, mem, nun, pe,* and *ṣade.* → Begad Kephat Letters.

**KENOSIS/KENOTIC.** From Greek *kenos,* "empty." A → christological term that refers to the self-limitation of Christ in the incarnation, derived from Phil. 2:5–11.

*Gk:* "but made himself nothing [lit., emptied himself], taking the very nature of a servant" (Phil. 2:7).

**KERNEL.** A sentence pattern that is basic to the structure of a language. There are six to eight kernels in each biblical language that can be transformed to derive all other sentence structures.

**KERYGMA.** Greek for "proclamation" or "preaching." A NT term for the act or content of apostolic proclamation of the gospel. The minimal points include (1) Jesus as the fulfillment of the OT promises, (2) His mission attested by mighty works, (3) His crucifixion, (4) resurrection, (5) ascension and promise of His → Parousia, and (6) a call to repentance issuing in the forgiveness of sins and the gifts of the Holy Spirit. *Ex:* Acts 2:14–39; 13:16–41; Rom. 1:1–6; 1 Cor. 15:1–8. In modern biblical theology and criticism, kerygma may refer to the content of what is preached or to the act of preaching.

**KETHIB.** The uncorrected word in the Hebrew text; the corrected word in the margin or footnote is the *qere. Heb:* 'ᵃnaû, kethib; 'ᵃnû, qere (Jer. 42:6).

**KETUBIM.** Hebrew name for the third division of the Hebrew Bible. See also → Hagiographa. → Torah, → Nebiim.

**KJV.** Abbreviation for *King James Version,* first published in 1611; it is frequently abbreviated KJ.

**KOHELETH.** Alternate spelling for → Qoheleth.

**KOINE GREEK.** The "common" Greek → dialect spread throughout the Greek East in the wake of Alexander's conquests, primarily through his armies; the → lingua franca of the → Hellenistic age. The NT is written in a Koine halfway between the → vernacular of the → papyri and the literary Koine of prose writers such as Josephus; the grammar and style owe much to the OT and can be described as Semitic or biblical Greek. → Semitism.

**KOINE TEXT.** Another name for the → Byzantine text.

**KOINONIA.** Greek for "fellowship."

**KOMPOSITIONSGESCHICHTE.** The German term for → composition criticism.

**KTL.** Usually written in Greek script. Abbreviation for *kai ta loipa*, "and the rest"; the Greek equivalent of ellipsis dots or *etc.* in English.

**KUNSTPROSA.** German for "artistic prose." Classical (Attic) Greek style created by sophists and rhetoricians ca. 400 B.C.; writings by a technically trained author that are intended to please the reader. According to F. Blass, in the NT only Hebrews fully qualifies as Kunstprosa.

# *L*

**L.** In OT → source criticism, a → siglum coined by Otto Eissfeldt to denote a "Lay" source that he believed should be distinguished from → J, → E, and → P. In source criticism of the Gospels, a siglum to designate the material unique to Luke. → Four Document Hypothesis.

**LABIALS.** The → mute consonants whose sounds are produced on the lips. In Hebrew, the labial consonants are *beth, mem,* and *pe.* In Greek they are *beta, pi,* and *phi.*

**LACUNA.** A gap or missing portion in a → manuscript.

**LAMED AUCTORIS.** A *lamed* prefixed to a word that indicates authorship or possession. *Heb: mizmôr l$^e$dāwid* (Ps. 23:1), "a psalm *of* David," but can also be understood as "a psalm *to/for* David."

**LAMENT.** A term used in → form criticism analysis to designate a particular literary form characterized by complaint or dirge; sometimes it is a funeral song. *Ex:* the Book of Lamentations.

**LAPIDARY.** Relating to that engraved on stone, hence a style of capital letters for use on stone monuments and → inscriptions.

**LARYNGEALS.** Another name for → gutturals.

**LASTERKATALOG.** German for "catalog of vices." → Ethical Lists.

**LATINISM.** A word or idiom derived from Latin that appears in the NT. The majority of occurrences are → loanwords from the areas of Roman administration, military, and coinage. *Gk: kolōnia* (Acts 16:12); *kentyriōn* (Mark 15:39); *dēnarion* (Matt. 20:9).

**LATTER PROPHETS.** In the Hebrew Bible, the designation of the books of the → major prophets and → minor prophets as distinguished from the → former prophets.

**LAW.** A general designation of the requirements of God to be obeyed by the covenant people. Specifically, it is the designation of the first five books of the Hebrew Bible, also called the → *Torah.* → Apodictic Law, → Casuistic Law.

**LB.** Abbreviation for *The Living Bible,* a paraphrase of the Scriptures published in its entirety in 1971.

**LECTIO BREVIOR.** Latin for "shorter reading." Used in → textual criticism to indicate a shorter → variant which, on principle, is often preferred (→ lectio potior).

**LECTIO DIFFICILIOR.** Latin for "more difficult reading." Used in → textual criticism to indicate the more difficult reading of a text.

**LECTIO FACILIOR.** Latin for "easier reading." Used in → textual criticism to indicate the easier reading of a text.

**LECTIO MARGINALIS.** Latin for "reading in the margin." Used in → textual criticism to indicate a reading of the text in the margin.

**LECTIONARY.** A compilation of portions of Scripture for use in worship services. Some NT scholars have sought the background of gospel and → epistolary forms in the lectionary cycles of Judaism; see → haftarah, → parash, and → seder. Greek lectionaries are valuable witnesses to the biblical text.

**LECTIO POTIOR.** Latin for "preferred reading." Used in → textual criticism to indicate the preferred reading of a text.

**LEGATOUR.** A stroke that is made accidentally in writing.

**LEGEND.** Popularly, a nonhistorical story, though it may be based on actual events. In → form criticism, used to describe a → genre that often evokes wonder and inspires religious devotion by its expression of truth; originally an oral story, developed and modified over a long period of time, that usually deals with holy men, holy places, or religious ceremonies.

**LEITMOTIV, LEITMOTIF.** A chief or repeated emphasis; it can be expressed through an extended → paronomasia. *Heb:* play on the consonants in the name "Noah" (Gen. 5:29; 6:6; 6:8; 8:4, 9, 21); the word "return" in Jer. 3–4. *Gk:* eleven occurrences of the "in Christ" theme (Eph. 1:3–14). → Motif.

**LEMMA.** Greek for "what is taken." The portion of text printed in a → critical apparatus for which evidence from manuscripts is cited; also a subtitle that gives the substance of the following text.

**LENINGRAD CODEX.** A Hebrew → manuscript of the entire OT copied in A.D. 1008, a primary witness to the → Ben Asher text. It forms the basis of *Biblia Hebraica* (→ BH) and *Biblia Hebraica Stuttgartensia* (→ BHS).

**LETTER.** The letters of Paul are closest in form to the familiar private correspondence of the → Hellenistic and Roman period. Their unique features include (1) apostolic greeting, (2) prayer report and thanksgiving, (3) an opening → formula to the main body, which itself consists of doctrine and → paraenesis, (4) a travelogue, and (5) a closing with Christian greetings. The distinction between letter and → epistle has limited value because some NT letters have the characteristics of public correspondence.

**LEVIRATE.** From Latin *levir*, "a husband's brother." A term used to describe the marriage laws of Deut. 25:5–10 that required a man to marry his deceased brother's wife under certain circumstances.

**LEVITE.** A member of the tribe of Levi, one of the original tribes of Israel that had engaged in military activities before being set apart for priestly functions (Gen. 34:25–30; 49:5; Exod. 32:26–29).

**LEXEME.** A minimal unit in the semantic system of a language, a word; a vocabulary entry in a Hebrew or Greek → lexicon.

**LEXICAL FORM.** The entry form under which the meaning of a word will be found in a → lexicon. Hebrew words are listed according to → root, usually the three → radicals of the consonantal root. Greek nouns are listed according to nominative, singular; verbs are listed according to present tense, indicative mood.

**LEXICON.** The word is used most frequently in biblical studies to designate a dictionary of Hebrew words that are found in the OT or a dictionary of Greek words that are found in the NT. *Ex:* Brown, Driver, and Briggs, *Hebrew and English Lexicon of the Old Testament;* Arndt, Gingrich, and Danker, *A Greek-English Lexicon of the New Testament and Other Early Christian Literature.* → Onomasticon.

**LEX TALIONIS.** Latin, "law of retaliation." Used for the law of retaliation ("an eye for an eye") of Exod. 21:24.

**LIBERTINISM.** Another term for → antinomianism.

**LIGATURE.** In → cursive writing, the stroke connecting two letters.

**LIGHT WAW.** Another name for → *waw* conjunctive.

**LINE.** → Stich.

**LINEAR.** An → aspect of the verb that depicts action in progress or continuing; also called *progressive* or *durative.* Usually expressed by the Hebrew and Greek → imperfect and the Greek → present. *Ex:* "I am walking" in contrast to "I walk."

**LINGUA FRANCA.** An auxiliary language used for routine communication between groups who speak different native languages. *Ex:* the use of → Aramaic in the ancient Near East; the use of → Koine in the Greek East.

**LINGUALS.** Another name for → dentals.

**LINGUISTICS.** The scientific study of language, developed as a discipline in the twentieth century; when the emphasis is historical, the term is equivalent to the older term → philology.

**LINKING VERB.** Another name for → copula.

**LIQUIDS.** A class of → consonants that are smooth, flowing sounds like → vowels. The liquids in Hebrew are *lamed, mem,* and *nun* and *resh;* in Greek they are *lambda* and *rho* and sometimes *mu* and *nu.*

**LITERAL.** The ordinary or basic meaning of a word or expression in contrast to a figurative meaning. → Figure, Figure of Speech.

**LITERAL TRANSLATION.** A translation that represents the exact or literal meaning of words. It usually retains the same word order of the original language as much as possible. An extremely literal translation from one language to another will frequently be awkward or unnatural. → Formal Equivalence.

**LITERARY CRITICISM.** A study of the literary characteristics

# LOCUS CLASSICUS

of a text, especially its structure, style, vocabulary, point of view, repetition of words, and logic. The distinction between the terms literary criticism and → source criticism is often confused by biblical scholars. See also → new literary criticism.

**LITERARY KOINE.** → Koine Greek.

**LITOTES.** A negative statement that is used to make an affirmative statement; also, an understatement that is used to increase the effect, the opposite of → hyperbole. Also called → *meiosis. Heb:* "A broken and contrite heart, O God, you will not despise" (Ps. 51:17). *Gk:* "I am not ashamed of the gospel" (Rom. 1:16a); "and they stayed there *a long time* [lit., no little time] with the disciples" (Acts 14:28).

**LOANWORD.** A foreign word used in a biblical text. There are, for example, Persian, Aramaic, and Greek loanwords found in the OT and Aramaic and Latin ones in the NT. *Heb:* a Persian word, *pardēs,* "orchard" (Song of Sol. 4:13). *Gk:* a Latin word, *phragellion,* "whip" (John 2:15).

**LOCAL TEXT.** A text form peculiar to a given locality. *Ex:* the Alexandrian text, allegedly the product of a revision by the Egyptian bishop Hesychius (died A.D. 307), found in Codex Vaticanus and Codex Sinaiticus.

**LOCATIVE CASE.** The → case that designates location, position, or sphere. In Hebrew it would usually be expressed by means of prepositions. In Greek it uses the same form as the → dative. *Heb:* "the entire army of Pharaoh that had followed the Israelites *into the sea*" (Exod. 14:28). *Gk:* "While Jesus was walking *in the temple*" (Mark 11:27).

**LOC. CIT.** Abbreviation of Latin *loco citato,* "in the place cited."

**LOCUS CLASSICUS.** A Latin term, used for the passage of

119

Scripture or other literature that is usually cited as the best illustration or explanation of a word or subject. *Ex:* John 3:16 is a *locus classicus* of the Gospel; Exod. 21:24 is the *locus classicus* for → lex talionis.

**LOGION (pl., LOGIA).** Greek for "saying." A saying of Jesus, usually in contrast to a longer utterance such as a → parable. *Gk:* "If anyone wants to be first, he must be the very last, and the servant of all" (Mark 9:35). The plural *logia* refers to a collection of sayings, particularly a sayings-source (→ Q) for the Gospels or the logia compiled by Matthew (according to Papias). See also → dominical saying.

**LOGOGRAM.** A sign that denotes a whole word. *Heb: yod* is frequently used for the divine name → Yahweh. *Gk: theta* for the divine name *Theos.*

**LOST SAYINGS.** → Agrapha.

**LOWER CRITICISM.** Another term for → textual criticism.

**LUCIANIC TEXT.** The revision of the Greek Bible ascribed to Lucian of Antioch (ca. A.D. 300); the basis of the → Byzantine text. Also called *Alpha, Antiochene, Syrian,* or *Koine text.*

**LXX.** Latin numerals for "seventy." Symbol for the → Septuagint. According to tradition, it was fitting that, since seventy elders accompanied Moses up Mount Sinai (Exod. 24:1–9), seventy elders should translate the → Torah into Greek. However, the *Letter of Aristeas* reasons that seventy-two were involved in the translation (six times twelve tribes).

**M.** In → source criticism of the Gospels, a → siglum to designate the unique material of Matthew. → Four Document Hypothesis.

**MAGIC.** A term used in biblical studies to describe a widespread belief in the ancient Near East that the gods could be activated or moved to work on behalf of a worshiper who brought offerings, performed prescribed rituals, or repeated certain incantations.

**MAGNALIA DEI.** Latin for "the mighty acts of God." The great deeds of God found in the Bible, such as the Exodus.

**MAGNIFICAT.** The name of Mary's hymn of praise at the announcement of Jesus' birth (Luke 1:46–55), derived from the opening word of the Latin text: *Magnificat anima mea Dominum*, "My soul praises the Lord."

**MAIN CLAUSE.** A → clause that stands on its own, not dependent on any other element. It can be a → sentence. Also called *independent* or *principal clause*. Heb. "When I appear, *they ridicule me*" (Job. 19:18). Gk: "If anyone loves the world, *the love of the Father is not in him*" (1 John 2:15). → Subordination.

**MAJOR PROPHETS.** In the Hebrew Bible, the books of Isaiah, Jeremiah, and Ezekiel. English Bibles (based on the → Septuagint arrangement) add the Book of Daniel; in the Hebrew Bible Daniel is found in the → Hagiographa.

**MAJUSCULE.** A large letter, capital letter, → uncial. → Minuscule.

**MAKARISM.** From Greek for "blessing." Another name for a beatitude (Matt. 5:3–10).

**MANUSCRIPT.** In → textual criticism this refers to the handwritten document in the original language. Secondarily, it is used to describe any handwritten document. It is abbreviated MS (sing.) and MSS (pl.).

**MAQQEPH.** A hyphenlike line that joins one or more Hebrew words that are closely associated in meaning. The word before the maqqeph loses its accent.

**MARANATHA.** A primitive → Aramaic → formula of the early church; the phrase can be translated as a → creedal declaration, "Our Lord has come" (*maran atha*), or, more likely, an eschatological prayer, "Our Lord, come!" (*marana tha*). *Gk:* 1 Cor. 16:22; cf. Rev. 22:20.

**MASHAL.** In the OT, a proverb or proverblike saying or story. It comes from a Hebrew word meaning "to be like" and forms the semantic background of the NT → parable. *Heb:* "Everyone who quotes *proverbs* will quote this *proverb* about you, 'Like mother, like daughter'" (Ezek. 16:44).

**MASORA FINALIS.** Information compiled by the → Masoretes that indicates the number of verses, the middle point, etc., in a given book of the OT.

**MASORA MAGNA.** Information found at the top and bottom margins of the Hebrew text; in general these notes provide supplements to the → masora parva.

**MASORA PARVA.** Information, found in the right and left

margins of the columns in the Hebrew text, concerning the external form of the text. The purpose of this information is to preserve the text unaltered.

**MASORETES.** From Hebrew for "tradition." The Jewish scholars who added the vowel points to the Hebrew consonantal text.

**MASORETIC TEXT.** The vocalized text of the Hebrew Bible, prepared by a group of Jewish scholars around A.D. 700 to preserve the oral pronunciation of the Hebrew words. → Masoretes.

**MASSORETES.** → Masoretes.

**MATRES LECTIONIS.** The letters (*he, waw, yod*) that represent vowels in an → unpointed text of the Hebrew Bible. Also called *fulcra or vowel letters.*

**MAXIM.** → Apothegm.

**MEGILLAH.** Singular of → Megilloth.

**MEGILLOTH.** The designation of five books of the OT that are read on Jewish religious holidays: Song of Solomon (Passover), Ruth (Pentecost), Lamentations (the ninth of Ab), Ecclesiastes (Tabernacles), and Esther (Purim).

**MEIOSIS.** In rhetoric, an understatement. Also called → *litotes.*

**MERISMUS.** Greek, "division into parts." A figure of speech related to → synecdoche in which a subject or topic is divided into its various parts. Two or more essential parts, often the first and last or the prominent contrasts (like "heaven and earth" = all creation), are mentioned, thereby indicating the genus or abstract quality that characterizes the whole. The extended form is called an *enumeration* or *series;* cf. Isa. 41:19; Jer. 7:9; Acts 2:8–11. *Heb:* "From the sole of your foot to the top of your head there is no soundness" (Isa. 1:6). *Gk:*

"Here there is no Greek or Jew, circumcised or uncircumcised, barbarian, Scythian, slave or free" (Col. 3:11).

**MESSIAH/MESSIANIC.** A title from a Hebrew word meaning "to smear," "to anoint." Kings and priests were anointed, i.e., set apart for their service through an anointing ceremony. The term came to be applied to a member of the family of David who would appear to restore the kingdom of Israel. The NT presents Jesus as the Christ (Greek *Christos* or Messiah), the fulfillment of the messianic hopes of the OT.

**MESSIANIC SECRET.** The intentional concealment of Jesus' identity as the → Messiah, particularly in Mark, by means of injunctions to silence following miracles (exorcisms and healings) and in training the twelve disciples. William Wrede argued that the secrecy → motif was Mark's invention, created to explain how Jesus could be proclaimed as the Messiah when he never claimed as much in his lifetime. The biblical motif is better described as a "Son of God" secret.

**METALANGUAGE.** Language about language, the formal terms or grammatical language used to describe language itself. *Ex:* sentence, clause, adjective, alliteration, etc.

**METAPHONE/METAPHONIC.** A word play in which a change of meaning is brought about by a change of vowels. *Heb:* šāqēḏ . . . šōqēḏ, "almond tree . . . watching" (Jer. 1:11–12). *Gk: limoi . . . loimoi,* "famines . . . pestilences" (Luke 21:11). → Annominatio, → Parachesis, → Paronomasia, Parasonancy.

**METAPHOR.** An implied comparison, the transfer of a descriptive term to an object to which it is not literally applicable; affirming that one thing "is" another. *Heb:* "The Lord *is* my light and my salvation" (Ps. 27:1). *Gk:* "I *am* the gate for the sheep" (John 10:7). → Parable, → Simile.

**METAPHRASE.** Word-for-word rendering of a text for pedagogical purposes; also a slavishly literal translation of the Bible. → Paraphrase.

**METAPLASM.** In Greek, the irregular → inflection of a noun that employs a different → stem in the → oblique cases. *Gk: sabbaton,* nominative; *sabbasin,* dative plural. → Heteroclisis.

**METATHESIS.** The transposition or reversal of letters (often consonants), words, or sentences. *Heb: kebeś* and *keśeb,* "lamb"; in the → hithpael → stem, when the first root letter of a verb is *samek* or *śin/šin,* metathesis occurs with the *taw* of the prefix, e.g., *hištammēr* instead of *hitšammēr. Gk: phailonēs* and *phainolēs,* "cloak."

**METER, METRE.** The systematically arranged and measured rhythm of poetry. The arrangement into feet (→ foot), syllabic groups, and accented and unaccented syllables are components of meter.

**METHEG.** A small, perpendicular stroke written under a Hebrew consonant and to the left of the vowel to indicate the secondary accent of a word, or the secondary accent of words joined with the → maqqeph.

**METHODOLOGY.** The form and methods of study employed in a given discipline.

**METONOMASIA.** The belief that a person's name symbolizes the self (or the soul) or that a new name would change the self or one's basic personality. Accordingly, the choice of names was important, and the changing of names was common in the ancient Near East. *Ex:* Jacob to Israel, Naomi to Mara, Simon to Peter.

**METONYMY.** The use of one word (often an attribute) for another that it suggests, as the effect for the cause, the cause for the effect, the sign for the thing signified. *Heb:* "You prepare a table before me" (Ps. 23:5); "table" is a metonym for food. *Gk:* "This cup is the new covenant in my blood" (Luke 22:20); "cup" is a metonym for its contents.

**METRE.** → Meter.

**MEZUZAH (pl., MEZUZOTH).** From Hebrew for "doorpost." A container placed on the doors of Jewish homes with copies of Deut. 6:4–9, 11:13–21. The custom developed from an interpretation given to the → Shema.

**MG.** Abbreviation of Latin *margo,* "margin." Used in → textual criticism for a reading in the margin of a → manuscript.

**MIDDLE VOICE.** The Greek → voice that calls attention to the agent or subject; sometimes equivalent to the Hebrew → reflexive, but more often an indirect, intensive way of stating the subject's involvement. It has the same form as the → passive, except in the → aorist tense → stem. *Gk:* "then I *shall know fully* [for myself], even as I am fully known" (1 Cor. 13:12).

**MIDDOT.** Hebrew for "measurements," "rules." Various collections of → exegetical principles (→ hermeneutics), drawn up by rabbis. The best known are the seven rules of Hillel. → Qal Waḥomer, → Gezerah Sawah.

**MIDRASH (pl., MIDRASHIM).** Rabbinic interpretation of the OT text, both the practice and → genre of rabbinic exposition. Its content may be either → halakic or → haggadic, although the best known midrashim (expository commentaries) are haggadic in nature. → Midrash Rabbah, → Tanḥuma, → Pesikta.

**MIDRASH RABBAH.** A collection of → haggadic → midrashim on the → Pentateuch and five → Megilloth; each of the ten sections is an independent composition, having its own character and date.

**MIL'EL.** In Hebrew, the accent on the next to the last syllable of a word; an accented → penult in Greek. → Paroxytone, → Properispomenon.

**MILLENNIALISM/MILLENNIAL.** Synonymous with → chiliasm/chiliastic.

**MILRAʿ.** In Hebrew, the accent on the last syllable of a word; an accented → ultima in Greek. → Oxytone, → Perispomenon.

**MINIMAL PAIR.** Two words that differ in only one sound, e.g., *pin* and *bin*. A useful device in learning the sounds of Hebrew and Greek.

**MINOR PROPHETS.** The twelve books of the prophets from Hosea to Malachi; the name originated with the rabbis.

**MINUSCULE.** Small letters joined together one after another with strokes. Also called → cursive writing. Minuscules, the → manuscripts of the Greek NT in this script, superseded the → uncial manuscripts and now form the great bulk of extant copies, more than 2500 manuscripts. → Majuscule.

**MISHNAH.** A codification of the traditional oral law of the → Tannaim as distinct from the written → Torah of the → Pentateuch. Committed to writing ca A.D. 200 by Rabbi Judah Ha-Nasi (The Prince); it is the basic → halakic document of Judaism, containing sixty-three → tractates organized into six major divisions. → Talmud.

**MI VERB.** A name for the → athematic Greek verb, derived from the ending -*mi* of the first person, singular, active voice.

**MNEMONIC DEVICE.** A literary aid to memory such as an → acrostic, catchword, or connected themes. *Heb:* the graded number in Amos' oracles against the nations—"for three crimes . . . and for four" (Amos 1:3, 6, 13; 2:1, 6). *Gk:* the arrangement of Jesus' genealogy into three sections of fourteen names, probably connected with the numerical value (→ gematria) of the name David in Hebrew: *dwd* = 14 (Matt. 1:1–17).

**MODAL.** A term that refers to some particular attitude (such as wish, possibility) toward the fulfillment of the action or state predicted, which may be expressed by → inflectional → mood, → auxiliary verbs, word order, etc. *Heb:* "God *may* yet relent" (Jonah 3:9).

**MODE.** Another term for → mood, although some grammarians distinguish the two (*mood* refers to the frame of mind in which the statement is made, *mode* to the manner in which it is made). *Mood* is more commonly used by Greek grammarians.

**MODIFIER.** A grammatical unit that limits or describes another word, → phrase, or → clause; usually it has an → adjectival or → adverbial function.

**MONOGENY.** Belief that the human race originated from one common ancestry, Adam and Eve.

**MONOGRAPH.** A scholarly, carefully documented study of a particular (usually limited) subject as opposed to an introduction or survey.

**MONOPHTHONG.** A single, pure vowel sound formed with the speech organs in a fixed position and articulated with no detectable change in quality. In Hebrew, → diphthongs may monophthongize except in closed, accented syllables and sometimes at the end of a word. In Greek, → itacism is the shift to the *i* monophthong.

**MONOTHEISM.** Belief in the existence of only one God.

**MOOD.** Mood indicates the manner in which the action is conceived (or its relation to reality). Moods are → indicative, → imperative, → subjunctive, and → optative. Mood may be expressed by → finite verbs in Greek and by various means (form, words, or context) in Hebrew. → Mode.

**MORPHEME.** The minimal functioning unit in the composition of words; a basic element or form of a language that shows grammatical relations, e.g., in English, an apostrophe and *s* to show possession. Morphemes are classified into bound forms (such as → affixes) and free forms that can occur as separate words. *Heb:* the *lamed* functioning as a prefixed preposition "to/for." *Gk: elue* comprises three morphemes, the prefix *e*, the stem *lu*, and the suffix *e*. → Phoneme.

**MORPHOLOGY.** A study of the forms (→ morphemes) that enter into the structure of words in a language. The → phoneme is the basic meaningful element of sound, the → morpheme the basic meaningful element of form. → Phonology.

**MOTIF.** In literature, a salient feature of the work, especially the recurring theme or dominant feature. It is any repetition that helps unify a work by recalling its earlier occurrence and all that surrounded it. *Heb:* the appeal to return to God is the motif of Jer. 3–4. *Gk:* the theme of God's righteousness pervades Paul's exposition in Rom. 3:21–5:21. → Leitmotiv.

**MOVABLE NU.** Out of a desire for → euphony, the (somewhat inconsistent) addition of Greek *nu* to words ending in -*si*, to the third person, singular suffix -*e*, and to the → copula *esti*.

**MS/MSS.** Abbreviations of → manuscript/manuscripts.

**MT.** Abbreviation for → Masoretic text.

**MU., MULT.** Abbreviations of Latin *multus*, "many." Used in a → critical apparatus to mean "many manuscripts read . . ."

**MULTIPLICATIVE.** A word formed with a → suffix to indicate multiplication of a quantity. *Heb:* the → dual suffix -*ayim: šibʿātayim*, "sevenfold." *Gk:* the suffix -*plous: diplous*, "twofold."

**MUTES.** A class of → consonants produced by a stoppage of breath in some part of the throat or mouth. Also called *stops* or *plosives.* There are ten mutes in Hebrew and nine in Greek. → Dentals, → Gutturals, → Labials.

**MYSTERY RELIGIONS.** The pagan cults of the → Hellenistic age whose adherents gained the promise of redemption by initiation into the secret ceremonies (Greek *mystē-rion,* "mystery") of the cults. The more important mystery religions were those of Isis and Osiris from Egypt, of Attis and Cybele from Phrygia in Asia Minor, of Adonis from Syria, of Mithras from Persia, and the Greek → cult of Demeter at Eleusis. → History of Religions School.

**MYTH.** Popularly, a story that is untrue, imaginative, or fictitious. In biblical studies the word has been applied in a positive and functional way (though misunderstood because of association with its popular meaning) to literary forms that express transcendent realities and truths in this-worldly terms. *Ex:* Some scholars say hell is not to be understood as a literal place (by this definition of myth), but as the human condition of being separated from God.

**MYTH AND RITUAL.** A school of biblical interpretation that applies certain insights from cultic knowledge gained from the study of comparative religions and then applied to biblical traditions. The centrality of the → cult, the character of sacred rites and festivals, sacral kingship, and the role of the king in cultic practices are special objects of interest of this school.

**MYTHOPOEIC.** The making of or giving rise to → myths.

**NAB.** Abbreviation for the *New American Bible*, a translation by Roman Catholic scholars published in 1970.

**NAG HAMMADI CODICES.** An extensive collection of fourth-century Christian and non-Christian → Gnostic writings, discovered in 1946 at a site near the modern city of Nag Hammadi in upper Egypt. The twelve → papyrus → codices represent many literary forms as well as diverse forms of → Gnosticism. The texts reinforce the view that Gnosticism has a non-Christian origin but does not predate the NT.

**NARRATIVE.** A type of → discourse basic to biblical literature; it is organized around a series of events in chronological order and includes participants and attendant circumstances. *Ex:* the Pentateuchal narratives of creation and Israel's early history.

**NASALS.** A class of → *consonants* produced by a closure of the breath passage in the mouth so that the air escapes through the nose. In Hebrew, the nasals are *mem* and *nun;* in Greek, *mu, nu,* and sometimes *gamma (yy* becomes *ng).*

**NASB.** Abbreviation for the *New American Standard Bible,* a revision of the *American Standard Version* (→ ASV), first published in its entirety in 1970.

**NASOG AHOR.** In Hebrew, the accent of the preceding word moves, under certain conditions, away from the accent that follows immediately, in order to avoid two successive heavy accents. Examples are found in Gen. 1:5, 4:17; Exod. 16:29.

**NEB.** Abbreviation for the *New English Bible*, a translation by British scholars, first published in its entirety in 1970.

**NEBIIM.** Hebrew name for the second division of the Hebrew Bible, the → Prophets. → Torah, → Ketubim.

**NEOPLATONISM.** A Greek philosophical system, centered in Alexandria in the third century A.D., developed by Ammonius Saccas, and expounded in writing by Plotinus, Porphyry, Iamblichus, and Proclus. Its antecedents included Platonism, Christianity, and → Gnosis.

**NESTLE-ALAND.** A critical text of the Greek NT, first published in 1898 by Eberhard Nestle; the 22nd–25th editions (1956–63) were revised by Erwin Nestle and Kurt Aland. The 26th edition (1979) and the third edition of the → United Bible Societies Greek NT print the same text with differences in punctuation and the critical apparatus.

**NEUTRAL TEXT.** A NT → text-type isolated by Westcott and Hort, based on → Codex Sinaiticus and → Codex Vaticanus. → Alexandrian Text.

**NEW LITERARY CRITICISM.** Another name for → structural analysis.

**NIKKUD.** → Pointing.

**NIPHAL.** A verbal form (→ stem) in Hebrew that expresses simple action and → passive or → reflexive voice. *Heb:* "She *was given* in marriage to Adriel of Meholah" (1 Sam. 18:19).

**NIV.** Abbreviation for the *New International Version,* a translation by evangelical scholars from several countries, first published in its entirety in 1978.

**NKJV.** Abbreviation for the *New King James Version,* a modernization of the → KJV, first published in its entirety in 1982.

**NOMEN RECTUM.** The noun (→ genitive) that describes an immediately preceding → nomen regens; in Hebrew this is the word that appears in the → absolute state. *Heb:* "the word of *the* Lord" (Jer. 1:2). *Gk:* "the kingdom *of God*" (Mark 1:15).

**NOMEN REGENS.** The noun that governs the → nomen rectum; in Hebrew this is the word that appears in the → construct. *Heb:* "*the word* of the Lord" (Jer. 1:2). *Gk:* "*the kingdom* of God" (Mark 1:15). A governing noun and its genitive are said to be *in regimen.*

**NOMINAL.** A term used by some grammarians for noun or declined forms of the noun pattern.

**NOMINAL SENTENCE.** A sentence is nominal if the → predicate does not contain a → finite verb. *Heb:* "For the Lord is our judge" (Isa. 33:22); there is no verb in the Hebrew. Commonly produced by → ellipsis in Greek.

**NOMINA SACRA.** Latin for "sacred names." The scribal practice in the earliest NT → manuscripts of abbreviating sacred names, e.g., God, Jesus, Son, Father, Spirit, Christ, Israel, and cross, often by contracting the name to its first and last letters with a line drawn above. *Gk:* *Christos* = $\overline{XC}$.

**NOMINATIVE ABSOLUTE.** → Casus Pendens.

**NOMINATIVE CASE.** The › case used primarily for the subject of a sentence and for the → subject complement. *Heb:* "Then *Moses* went up to God" (Exod. 19:3). *Gk:* "*I* am the true *vine*" (John 15:1).

**NONCANONICAL.** Another term for → extracanonical.

**NONFINITE VERB.** → Finite Verb.

**NONRESTRICTIVE.** A phrase or clause that can be set off by a comma or commas because it is nonessential, i.e., it could be omitted without changing the meaning of the main clause. *Heb:* "This girl, *who was also known as Esther*, was lovely in form and features" (Esth. 2:7). *Gk:* "On the eighth day, *when it was time to circumcise him*, he was named Jesus" (Luke 2:21).

**NOTARIKON.** A rabbinic term for an → acronym.

**NOUN.** A noun is the name of a person, place, idea, or thing. A *proper noun* names a particular person, place, idea, or thing (e.g., Joseph, Jerusalem). A *common noun* is one that names any of a class of beings or things (shepherd, city). An *abstract noun* names a quality, activity, or state that is considered apart from any particular being or thing (e.g., peace, righteousness), in contrast to a *concrete noun* (e.g., house, sun). → Collective Noun.

**NOUN PHRASE.** In → generative grammars, the complete subject with all its → modifiers.

**NOVELLA.** In → form criticism, a term used to describe what could be called a novelette or short story.

**NUMBER.** In → parsing of words in Greek or Hebrew, this term is used to show whether the word refers to one or more than one person, place, or thing. In Hebrew there are three numbers: singular, plural, and dual; in Greek there are two: singular and plural.

**NUMISMATICS.** The study and collection of coins.

**NUNC DIMITTIS.** The name of Simeon's prayer at the dedication of Jesus (Luke 2:29–32), derived from the first two words of the Latin text: *Nunc dimittis servum tuum*, "now dismiss your servant."

**NUN DEMONSTRATIVUM.** Latin name for → energic *nun*.

**NUN ENERGICUM.** Latin name for → energic *nun*.

**NUN EPENTHETICUM.** Latin name for → energic *nun*.

# O

**OBJECT COMPLEMENT.** A word or phrase that completes the meaning of the → direct object, usually after → factitive verbs. Also called *predicate accusative* or *objective complement*. *Heb:* "So he named him *Israel*" (Gen. 35:10). *Gk:* "I no longer call you *servants*" (John 15:15).

**OBJECTIVE GENITIVE.** The noun or possessive pronoun in the genitive is the object of the relationship expressed. *Heb:* "visions of God" = "to see God" (Ezek. 1:1). *Gk:* "blasphemy of the Spirit" (Matt. 12:31) = "blasphemy against the Spirit."

**OBLIQUE CASES.** All Greek → case forms except the nominative and the vocative (called direct cases). Because Hellenistic grammarians regarded the nominative as the "upright case" (*ptōsis orthē*), the genitive-ablative, dative-locative-instrumental, and accusative forms "slant" from it; thus, they are called oblique.

**OCTATEUCH.** The first eight books of the OT (counting 1–2 Samuel as one book and omitting Ruth).

**OCTAVO.** In printing, a sheet folded three times and cut to produce eight leaves, or the size of a book made of sheets folded three times; the result is sixteen pages to a sheet. Abbreviated 8vo or 8°. → Folio, → Quarto.

**OG.** Abbreviation for → Old Greek.

**OLD GREEK.** The earliest pre-Christian translations of the Bible into Greek, most likely made in Egypt, also called *Proto-LXX.* → Proto-Lucian.

**OLD LATIN.** A second century A.D. translation of the → Septuagint into Latin; also known as *Itala* and *Vetus Latina.*

**OM.** Abbreviation of Latin *omittit* or *omittunt,* "it omits," "they omit." Used in a → critical apparatus to mean "this reading omitted" in a → manuscript or manuscripts.

**OMEGA VERB.** A name for the → thematic verb in Greek, derived from the ending -ō of the first person, singular, active voice.

**OMN.** Abbreviation of Latin *omnes,* "all." Used in a → critical apparatus to mean "all manuscripts read . . ."

**OMNIFICENCE/OMNIFICENT.** A word that describes God as the Creator of all things.

**ONOMASTICON (pl., ONOMASTICA)/ONOMASTIC.** Pertains to a name or names. It may designate an autograph signature or a document written by someone else. It may be a list of names, especially proper names, of people, places, or occupations, given as an aid to their meaning or → etymology. Formerly used for → lexicon or dictionary. *Ex:* 1 Chron. 11:26–47.

**ONOMATOPOEIA/ONOMATOPOEIC.** The sound of the word suggests its meaning: "buzz" and "hiss" are onomatopoeic words. *Heb:* the word for "serpent," *nāhāš,* suggests a hissing sound. *Gk:* the word for "complaining," *gongusmos,* suggests a grumbling sound.

**OPISTOGRAPH.** A → papyrus roll with text written also on

the → verso or "outside" (Greek, *opisthen*). *Heb:* "On both sides of it were written words" (Ezek. 2:10). *Gk:* "a scroll with writing on both sides" (Rev. 5:1).

**OPTATIVE MOOD.** The → mood of possibility and more doubtful assertion that expresses wish or desire. See also → jussive and → cohortative. *Heb: "If only we had died* in Egypt!" (Num. 14:2). *Gk: "May* the Lord *direct* your hearts into God's love and Christ's perseverance" (2 Thess. 3:5).

**ORACLE.** A term used to mean any communication or message from God to man.

**ORAL TRADITION.** The preliterary stages of a written text; the assumption that a spoken message passed from generation to generation by word of mouth before taking a fixed written form. *Ex:* individual → pericopes in the Gospels. → Form Criticism, → Tradition Criticism.

**ORAL TRADITIONAL LITERATURE.** In contrast to the phrase → oral tradition, a → genre of unwritten literature, epic poetry, and → narrative by which a song or story is transmitted in patterns that have both stability and variation. The researches of Parry and Lord in this literature have been applied to Gospel studies.

**ORATIO OBLIQUA.** A Latin term for → indirect discourse.

**ORATIO RECTA.** A Latin term for → direct discourse.

**ORDINAL.** Short for ordinal number (first, second, third, etc.). → Cardinal.

**ORIGINAL GOSPEL.** → Urevangelium.

**ORIGINAL MARK.** → Urmarkus.

**ORTHOGRAPHY.** The correct writing of words and letters according to standard usage.

**ORTHOPHONICUM.** In Hebrew, a → *daghesh lene* that appears in a consonant other than a → begad kephat letter. Its purpose is to call attention expressly to the beginning of a new syllable. *Heb: lô lō':* a dagesh lene appears in the second *lamed;* see also Deut. 32:6, 15.  ʹ

**OSTRACON (pl., OSTRACA).** Unglazed pottery pieces (potsherds), used as a writing material in the ancient Near East.

**OTIANT ALEPH.** A final *aleph* preceded by a simple → *shewa* in Hebrew.

**OTIOSE.** A grammatical form that lacks use, effect, or function; see also → pleonasm. *Ex:* the redundant participle *saying* in biblical narrative (*lêmōr* in Hebrew, *legōn* in Greek): "he said, saying. . . ."

**OXYMORON.** The placing together of contradictory or incongruous terms for → epigrammatic effect. *Heb:* "living water" (Jer. 2:13). *Gk:* "living stones" (1 Peter 2:5).

**OXYRHYNCHUS PAPYRI.** A large number of ancient papyrus fragments found at Oxyrhynchus in Upper Egypt that date from the second century B.C. to the seventh century A.D. Written in several languages, they include fragments of biblical texts.

**OXYTONE.** In Greek a word with the acute accent on the → ultima. → Barytone, → Paroxytone.

# P

**P.** Abbreviation for the Priestly source. → JEDP.

**PALATALS.** Another name for → gutturals.

**PALEOGRAPHY.** The study of ancient writing as a means for dating and deciphering texts.

**PALESTINIAN TALMUD.** → Gemara.

**PALIMPSEST.** A → parchment from which writing was erased to make room for another text.

**PALINDROME.** A type of → anagram, a word or sentence which may be read backwards as well as forwards, letter by letter, without a change in meaning. *Ex: tenet. Heb: sûs,* "horse."

**PANEGYRIC.** A discourse or poem in praise of an individual, institution, or class of people. Originally a → genre of Greek rhetoric, laudatory discourse flourished among authors of the Roman period. Sections of Paul's letters approach such a style. *Heb:* Exod. 15:1–18, the Song of Moses at the Sea of Reeds. *Gk:* Eph. 1:3–3:21. → Encomium, → Epideictic Oratory, → Second Sophistic.

**PAPPONYMY.** The practice in the ancient Near East of giving a child the same name as his grandfather.

**PAPYRUS (pl., PAPYRI).** An Egyptian plant made into a writing material (hence called papyrus) by the ancient Egyptians and widely used by other ancient peoples. Sheets were formed by cutting the stems into long, thin strips that were placed in two crosswise layers and glued together by hammer blows.

**PAR.** In → Gospel criticism, an abbreviation for "and its parallel," referring to a parallel passage in one or more of the Gospels.

**PARABLE/PARABOLIC.** A short, usually fictitious, → narrative in which a moral or spiritual truth is taught; an extended → metaphor. In the teaching of Jesus it takes the form of a story or anecdote, an → aphorism, or a → similitude. The primary meaning of the kingdom of God is spoken in parables. *Heb:* Isa. 5:1–7. *Gk:* Parable of the Mustard Seed (Matt. 13.31–32).

**PARABLEPSIS.** Greek for "looking to the side." An error made by a → copyist when his eye returned to the wrong line in the text. It is an error that is easy to make when two adjacent lines begin or end with the same word. → Homoioteleuton.

**PARACHESIS.** A form of → paronomasia that uses different words of similar sound. *Gk: asunetous, asunthetous,* "senseless, faithless" (Rom. 1:31). → Annominatio, → Metaphone, → Parasonancy.

**PARADIGM.** An example or pattern of a → conjugation or → declension, showing a word in all its → inflectional forms. In → form criticism, another name for → apothegm.

**PARADOSIS.** Greek for "tradition." A technical term in the NT for the transmission and content of kerygmatic and ethical traditions in the apostolic circle. *Gk:* 2 Thess. 2:15. → Didache, → Kerygma, → Paraenesis.

**PARADOX.** A statement that is self-contradictory or seemingly false or opposed to common sense, but which in fact may be profoundly true; e.g., the sovereignty of God does not preclude human freedom. Biblical language and faith is replete with such paradox. *Heb:* "Those who guide this people mislead them, and those who are guided are led astray" (Isa. 9:16). *Gk:* "For when I am weak, then I am strong" (2 Cor. 12:10).

**PARAENESIS/PARAENETIC, PARENESIS/PARENETIC.** In → form criticism, used to describe a text containing a series of admonitions, usually ethical and eclectic in nature; it exhorts or gives advice. *Heb:* Prov. 1:8–19. *Gk:* 1 Thess. 4:1–12. → Household Codes.

**PARAGOGIC.** In Hebrew, the paragogic *nun* ending (-*ûn*) is found instead of the usual plural ending (-*û*) over three hundred times. There is also a paragogic *he* (also called *emphatic he*). Paragogic *nun* and *he* usually express marked emphasis; however, the paragogic *nun* may sometimes be used for → euphony. *Heb:* "tremble" (Exod. 15:14; paragogic *nun*). → Euphonic Nun.

**PARALEIPOMENON.** Name given by the Greek translators of the → Septuagint to 1–2 Chronicles. The word means "things omitted," i.e., not found in the parallel account in 1–2 Samuel and 1–2 Kings.

**PARALIPSIS.** A rhetorical figure in which the author pretends to pass over something which he in fact mentions. *Gk:* "we—not to say anything about you—would be ashamed of having been so confident" (2 Cor. 9:4).

**PARALLEL.** A word, idea, or construction that is similar in all essential points to another. *Heb:* For you have been my *refuge, a strong tower* against the foe" (Ps. 61:3). *Gk:* "he will give you another *Counselor* . . . the *Spirit of truth*" (John 14:16–17). → Parallelism.

**PARALLELISM.** In Hebrew poetry, the relationship between two or more lines. Hebrew poetry is characterized by parallelism of thought rather than by rhyme. The types of parallelism that have been identified in Hebrew poetry include: → synonymous, → synthetic, → antithetic, → emblematic, → inverted (chiastic), and → climactic.

**PARALLELISMUS MEMBRORUM.** A Latin term that refers to the parallelism between lines of Hebrew poetry. → Parallelism.

**PARAPHRASE/PARAPHRASTIC.** Restatement of a text, passage, or literary composition, giving the meaning in words other than those of the original writer or speaker. Also, a free translation. Do not confuse with → periphrasis. *Ex: The Living Bible* is a paraphrase rather than a → translation. → Dynamic Equivalence, → Metaphrase.

**PARASH (pl., PERASHOTH, PERASHIYOTH).** The sections into which Babylonian Jews divided the → Torah, to be read weekly in worship services over a one-year period. The beginning of a parash may be indicated by the letters *pe, resh, sin* in the margin of the Hebrew text or by the letter *pe* written three times in the text gap. → Seder.

**PARASONANCY.** A wordplay brought about by a change of consonants in verbal or nominal roots. *Heb: ṣᵉdāqāh . . . ṣᵉʿāqāh*, "righteousness . . . distress" (Isa. 5:7). *Gk: phthonou phonou*, "envy, murder" (Rom. 1:29). → Paronomasia.

**PARATAXIS.** Coordination of words, → clauses, and/or sentences in series, without any other expression of their syntactical relationship; the opposite of → hypotaxis or → subordination. It is characteristic of Hebrew composition (→ copulative waw) and appears in sections of the NT influenced by Semitic style. *Gk:* copulative *kai* at the beginning of Mark's → pericopes. → Coordinate/ Coordination.

**PARCHMENT.** A writing material prepared from the skins of animals. → Vellum.

**PARENESIS.** → Paraenesis.

**PARENTHESIS.** A grammatically independent thought placed in the middle of a sentence; an afterthought that interrupts the structure of the sentence. *Heb:* long parentheses followed by → anacoluthon (Num. 14:21–23; Deut. 17:2–5). *Gk:* "I planned many times to come to you (*but have been prevented from doing so until now*) in order that I . . ." (Rom. 1:13).

**PARONOMASIA.** A play on words; a pun using similar sounds with different sense. *Heb:* "I see the branch of an almond tree [*šāqēḏ*] . . . I am watching [*šōqēḏ*]" (Jer. 1:11–12). *Gk:* "He learned [*emathen*] obedience from what he suffered [*epathen*]" (Heb. 5:8). → Annominatio, → Metaphone, → Parachesis, → Parasonancy.

**PAROUSIA.** Greek for "coming," "presence." Used in the NT as a → common noun, e.g., "comforted by the *coming* of Titus" (2 Cor. 7:6), but primarily as a technical term for the return of Christ. *Gk:* "Concerning the *coming* of our Lord Jesus Christ" (2 Thess. 2:1).

**PAROXYTONE.** In Greek, a word with the acute accent on the → penult. → Barytone, → Oxytone.

**PARSE/PARSING.** A pedagogical exercise to aid in → morphological analysis; to describe grammatically a part of speech by listing its → inflectional modifications and/or its → syntactic relationships in the sentence. *Heb:* The verb '*āmar* would be parsed as *qal*, perfect, third person, masculine gender, and singular in number. *Gk:* the verb *lusomen* is future, active, indicative, first, plural. → Analytical Lexicon.

**PARSING GUIDE.** → Analytical Lexicon.

**PARTICIPLE.** A verbal form that has characteristics of both noun and verb. In Hebrew it represents characteristic, continual, uninterrupted action. *Heb:* "The Spirit of

God *was hovering* over the waters" (Gen. 1:2). The Greek participle is widely used as a → substantive, → adjective, and → adverb in → phrases and → clauses. *Gk:* ". . . in God, *who raised* him from the dead and *glorified* him" (1 Peter 1:21).

**PARTICIPIAL NOUN.** Another name for → gerund.

**PARTICLE.** A unit of speech that is ranked as an uninflected word but expresses some kind of syntactical relationship or some general aspect of meaning. Some grammarians classify all conjunctions, prepositions, and negatives as particles.

**PARTITIVE.** A word that divides into parts: a word in the → genitive case that names the whole from which a part is taken. *Heb:* the partitive genitive can express the superlative degree with *min* (e.g., wise men *from the men* = wisest of the men). *Min,* "from," is a partitive word; it can also mean "some" (e.g., *from* the men = some of the men). *Gk:* "one *of these,*" "a tenth *of the city*" (partitive genitives).

**PARTS OF SPEECH.** The major word classes into which the vocabulary of a language is divided. Traditional divisions in Hebrew and Greek grammar are based on meaning and function; they are → noun, → pronoun, → adjective, → verb, → adverb, → preposition, → conjunction, and → particle.

**PASSIVE VOICE.** A → *voice* form of the verb that represents the subject as receiver of the action. *Heb:* "This land *was given* to us as our possession" (Ezek. 11:15). *Gk:* "You *were marked* in him with a seal" (Eph. 1:13).

**PASSIVUM DIVINUM.** A passive verb construction with an indefinite agent who from the context can be identified as God; a biblical adaptation (→ Semitism) of the → impersonal verb or → indefinite plural to avoid using the divine name. *Heb:* "For the power of the wicked will be broken, but the LORD upholds the righteous" (Ps. 37:17). *Gk:* "Give, and it will be given to you. A good measure . . . will be poured into your lap" (Luke 6:38). → Antonomasia.

**PASTORAL EPISTLES.** Since the eighteenth century a collective name for 1–2 Timothy and Titus, owing to their nature as pastoral instruction for church ministry.

**PAST PERFECT TENSE.** → Pluperfect Tense.

**PATOIS.** A → dialect spoken by the common people in a geographical region and materially different from the literary language. *Ex:* Palestinian → Aramaic and vernacular → Koine.

**PATRISTICS.** From Latin *pater,* "father." The branch of theological study that deals with the writings and thought of the Greek and Latin church fathers; in a stricter sense, the major Christian fathers to the close of the eighth century A.D. Also called *patrology.*

**PATROLOGY.** Another name for → patristics.

**PATRONYMIC.** A name formed by the addition of a → prefix or → suffix indicating relationship or descent (e.g., Johnson = "John's son"). Hebrew patronymics are formed by → gentilic endings. *Heb:* Moabite, Israelite. *Gk:* Herodias, "daughter of Herod."

**PAUC.** → PC.

**PAUSE.** In Hebrew, the last word in a sentence (marked by an accent called a *silluq*), or the last word in the first major division of a sentence (marked by an accent called an *athnaḥ*), is said to be in pause.

**P.C., PAUC.** Abbreviations of Latin *pauci,* "few." Used in a → critical apparatus to mean "a few manuscripts read."

**PEDILAVIUM.** Latin for "washing of feet" (see John 13).

**PENDENS.** A suspended, grammatical construction. → Casus Pendens.

**PENTATEUCH.** Greek name for the first five books of the OT.

**PENTATEUCHAL CRITICISM.** The application of various methods of critical analysis (→ criticism) to the first five books of the OT.

**PENULT, PENULTIMA.** In Greek, the next to the last syllable of a word; when accented, called the → mil'el in Hebrew. → Paroxytone, → Properispomenon.

**PERFECTIVE.** An → aspect of the verb that indicates completion of an action or state; see also → effective aorist.

**PERFECT OF CERTAINTY.** The technical name for → prophetic perfect.

**PERFECT/PERFECT TENSE.** In Hebrew, this form of the verb is used to express completed action, whether in reality or in the thought of the speaker or writer. *Heb:* šāmar is a perfect form of the verb and would be translated "he guarded." The Greek perfect → tense, by contrast, represents a state of completion with abiding results and is often translated as a present perfect. *Gk:* The perfect *leluke* would be rendered "he has released."

**PERFORMATIVE UTTERANCE.** A term coined by J. E. Austin and now found in → semantics to describe a sentence where an action is performed by virtue of the sentence having been uttered. *Ex:* "I promise." *Heb:* "Out of the depths I cry to you, O LORD" (Ps. 130:1). *Gk:* "Friend, your sins are forgiven" (Luke 5:20).

**PERICOPE.** A designated portion or unit of Scripture; it may be quite brief or relatively long. Particularly, the self-contained literary units or sections of the Gospels. *Heb:*

Ezek. 18:15–17 is a pericope. *Gk:* the healing of the paralytic in Capernaum (Mark 2:1–12).

**PERICOPE DE ADULTERA.** The passage concerning the woman taken in adultery, found in most versions of John's Gospel (John 7:53–8:11). It is an ancient → interpolation with good claim to authenticity but is not found in the earliest → manuscripts of John.

**PERIODIC SENTENCE.** A longer → complex sentence, organized into a well-rounded unity, usually with balanced or → antithetical phrases and exhibiting clear syntactical relationship; by classical definition the verb comes last. Found only in the more literary prose of the NT. *Gk:* the → prologue to Luke's Gospel (Luke 1:1–4).

**PERIPETEIA, PERIPETIA, PERIPETY.** A term used in literary analysis to describe a sudden or unexpected turn of events or reversal of circumstances. *Heb:* "You are the man!" (2 Sam. 12:7); the Book of Esther. *Gk:* 2 Cor. 10–13; vision and interlude in the Book of Revelation.

**PERIPHRASIS/PERIPHRASTIC.** A roundabout expression (→ circumlocution). *Heb:* "man of lips" = "talker" (Job 11:2); "men of strength" = "best fighting men" (Josh. 8:3). *Gk:* used especially for a → tense composed of an → auxiliary verb and a → participle (periphrastic tense) that is used instead of a simple tense: *ēn didaskōn* for *edidasken*, "he taught [lit., was teaching] them" (Mark 1:22). Do not confuse with → paraphrase.

**PERISPOMENON.** In Greek, a word with the circumflex accent on the → ultima.

**PERMUTATION.** A variety of → apposition; it is not complementary like apposition but rather defines the preceding → substantive (or pronoun); also used for → commutation. *Heb:* "saw it, the child" = "saw the baby" (Exod. 2:6).

**PERSON.** Denotes the speaker or the person or thing spoken to or about. There are three persons in English, Greek, and Hebrew: first ("I/we"); second ("you"); and third ("he, she, it/they").

**PERSONAL ENDINGS.** In Greek, the verb suffixes that indicate person and number; comparable to → pronominal suffixes in Hebrew.

**PERSONIFICATION.** A figure of speech in which some human characteristic is attributed to an inanimate or abstract object. *Heb:* "The *land* we explored *devours* those living in it" (Num. 13:32). *Gk:* "the *stones* will *cry out*" (Luke 19:40).

**PESACH, PESAH.** The Hebrew name for Passover.

**PESHER (pl., PESHERIM).** Hebrew for "commentary." A unique form of → haggadic › midrash documents found among the → Dead Sea Scrolls. The commentary form uses a → formula, "this means," and fulfillment → motif revealing the mystery of God's purpose. *Ex:* the Habbakuk commentary from Qumran (abbreviated 1 QpH).

**PESHITTA.** A translation of the OT and NT into the → Syriac language. → Syriac Versions.

**PESIKTA (pl., PESIKTOT).** Hebrew for "section." A collection of → midrashim linked with Jewish festivals and special sabbaths. *Ex: Pesikta Rabbati* is a compilation of forty-eight → homilies, probably from the seventh century A.D.

**PETHUCA.** In the Hebrew Bible, an open paragraph, indicated by a *pe* in the text. → Setuma.

**PETITIO PRINCIPII.** Latin for "begging the question." A form of circular argument in which what is to be proved is implicitly taken for granted.

**PHENICIAN.** → Phoenician.

**PHILOLOGY.** Traditional term for the study of language history; in the widest sense, the study of literature, also → linguistics; in classical usage, the study of ancient culture as revealed in history, language, art, literature, and religion.

**PHOENICIAN.** A people who lived on the Mediterranean coastal plain from Byblos to Tyre and Sidon; also the name of the language spoken by these people.

**PHONEME.** The minimal unit of speech sound in a given language that distinguishes one utterance from another. *Heb:* the *he* in *hāyāh,* "to be," and the *heth* in *ḥāyāh,* "to live," distinguish these words from each other. *Gk:* the *p* in *pōs,* "how," and the *ph* in *phōs,* "light," distinguish these two words from each other.

**PHONEMICS.** Analysis of different sounds that affect meaning; the branch of → linguistics that deals with → phonemes.

**PHONETICS.** The science of speech sounds as elements of a language; the study of the characteristics of human soundmaking.

**PHONOGRAM.** Writing in which the sound conveys the meaning. *Ex:* a picture of the sun = "son."

**PHONOLOGY.** Deals with the → phonemic and → phonetic elements of a language; these elements roughly correspond to the consonants and vowels. It also deals with accents, syllabification, consonantal and vocalic alterations, and similar phenomena. It is that part of the grammar of a language that describes its sounds and sound changes. → Morphology.

**PHRASE.** A group of words that functions as a → substantive or → modifier but lacks the → subject and → predicate typical of a → clause. *Heb:* "He was assigned a grave *with the wicked*" (Isa. 53:9). *Gk:* "Then, *leaving* *her water jar*, the woman went back to the town" (John 4:28).

**PHYLACTERY.** → Tephillah.

**PICTOGRAM.** Writing that is represented by pictures; in contrast to the → ideogram, the meaning of the pictogram is limited to the thing depicted. Also called *pictograph*.

**PICTOGRAPH.** → Pictogram.

**PIEL.** A verbal form in Hebrew that expresses intensive or emphatic action and active → voice. *Heb:* "They *destroyed* the high places and the altars" (2 Chron. 31:1).

**PIRQE ABOTH.** "The Chapters of the Fathers." The title of the oldest → tractate of the → Mishnah, a collection of sayings, mostly moral → aphorisms, of some sixty → Tannaim, arranged chronologically. Because of its ethical and literary significance, it is still read on different occasions as part of Jewish liturgy.

**PIZKA.** A space in the Hebrew text that marks a division into two separate sections. *Heb:* after Isa. 1:9.

**PL., PLER.** Abbreviations of Latin *plerique*, "very many." Used in a → critical apparatus to mean "very many manuscripts read . . . ."

**PLAY ON WORDS.** → Paronomasia.

**PLENA.** Latin for "full." When the originally long vowel is written with its vowel letters, it is said to be written fully (*plena* writing) Also called *full writing, scriptio plena*, or *plene writing.* → Defective Writing.

**PLENARY INSPIRATION.** From Latin, "full." The view that the Bible is inspired in all its parts. Frequently used synonymously with → verbal inspiration.

**PLENE WRITING.** Another name for → plena writing.

**PLEONASM/PLEONASTIC.** Redundant use of words or an unnecessary addition such as a pleonastic → *waw* or a pleonastic participle. *Heb:* "*And* the word of the Lord came to Jonah" (Jonah 1:1). *Gk:* "He replied," lit., "answering, he said" (Luke 20:3). → Otiose, → Tautology.

**PLOSIVES.** Another name for → mutes.

**PLUPERFECT TENSE.** A verbal tense that expresses action completed before another action in the past or a state following a completed act in past time; it occurs infrequently in the NT. Also called the *past perfect tense.* *Heb:* "The Lord was grieved that he *had made* man on the earth" (Gen. 6:6). *Gk:* "By now it was dark, and Jesus *had not* yet *joined* them" (John 6:17).

**POIMANDRES.** → Hermetic Literature.

**POINTING.** A term that refers to the vowels added by the → Masoretes to the consonantal text of the OT (Hebrew was originally written without vowels) in order to preserve the pronunciation of the language at a time when it was in danger of being forgotten. It is also called *nikkud.*

**POLYGLOT.** A book that contains in columns side by side a number of versions of the same text in several languages. Some well-known polyglots include the → *Hexapla* of Origen and the *Complutensian Polyglot.*

**POLYPHONE.** A single sign with a number of different phonetic values. *Ex:* the letter *e* in English.

**POLYSEMY.** The phenomenon of a word that has developed two or more entirely distinct meanings. *Ex: pupil* of the eye, a school *pupil. Heb:* The word 'āšām can mean "sin" or "sin offering." *Gk: peirasmos* can mean "temptation" or "test."

**POLYSYNDETON.** The repetition of conjunctions in a series of coordinate words or phrases; polysyndeton is quite typical of Hebrew. *Heb: waw,* "and," is used six times in Gen. 12:16. *Gk: kai,* "and," is used six times in Rev. 7:12. → Asyndeton.

**POLYTHEISM.** The belief in more than one god.

**POSITIVE DEGREE.** The basic form of the adjective or adverb; it does not express comparison, in contrast to the → elative and the → comparative and → superlative degrees. *Heb:* "I will make you into a *great* nation" (Gen. 12:2). *Gk:* "A *good* tree cannot bear *bad* fruit" (Matt. 7:18).

**POSTAPOSTOLIC AGE.** The period immediately following the → apostolic age, ca. A.D. 100–150; also called *sub-upostolic age.*

**POSTPOSITIVE.** Greek words, mostly → particles, that cannot stand first in a clause or sentence and are usually in second position. *Gk:* commonly, *gar,* "for," *oun,* "therefore," and *de,* "but."

**POTSHERD.** → Ostracon.

**PRECATIVE MOOD.** Another name for → optative. → Jussive, → Cohortative.

**PREDICATE.** The verb together with its → modifiers and → complements; sometimes called → *verb phrase.* Forms that appear among the complements and modifiers are described as predicate, e.g., predicate accusative.

**PREDICATE ADJECTIVE.** In Greek, the → subject complement.

**PREDICATE ACCUSATIVE.** In Greek, the → object complement.

**PREDICATE COMPLEMENT.** → Complement.

**PREDICATE NOMINATIVE.** In Greek, the → subject complement.

**PREDICATE NOUN.** In Greek, the → subject complement.

**PREFIX.** An inflectional → affix; one or more letters or syllables placed at the beginning of a → root or → stem in Greek and Hebrew that will modify its meaning. Also called a *preformative*. *Heb:* prefix *nun* to form the → niphal stem. *Gk:* the → reduplicated prefix to form the → perfect tense.

**PREFORMATIVE.** Another term for → prefix.

**PREFORMATIVE CONSONANT.** In Hebrew, this term refers to the consonants that characteristically appear with the imperfect forms of the Hebrew verb (*yod, tav, aleph,* and *nun*); it may refer to any consonant → prefixed to the → root.

**PREFORMATIVE VOWEL.** In Hebrew, this term refers to the vowel that characteristically appears with the → preformative consonant and helps identify the → stem of the verbal form. → Prefix.

**PREGNANT CONSTRUCTION.** A construction that implies more than the words say explicitly; also called *constructio praegnans*. Common in Greek prepositions after verbs of motion or rest; a form of → brachylogy. *Heb:* "They turned to each other trembling" (Gen. 42:28), lit., "they trembled, each to his brother." *Gk:* "They were baptized by him *in* the Jordan River" (Matt. 3:6), i.e., they were baptized *into* and were *in* the river. cf. Mark 1:9.

**PRE-MASORETIC.** Another name for → proto-Masoretic.

**PREPOSITION.** A word that shows relationships between its object and some other word in the sentence. Some common English prepositions are *in, to, from, with, above, for, by.*

**PREPOSITIONAL PHRASE.** The phrase that includes the preposition and its object. *Ex: to the city.*

**PRESENT TENSE.** The Greek present → tense depicts the action of the verb as → linear or progressive, a continuing activity in present time (in the → indicative mood). The Hebrew → imperfect is often its equivalent. *Heb:* "What *are* you *looking* for?" (Gen. 37:15). *Gk:* "He *is going* ahead of you into Galilee" (Mark 16:7).

**PRETERITE.** A Latin name for the past tense; it is the equivalent of the → perfect in Hebrew and the → aorist indicative in Greek.

**PRETONIC.** The syllable immediately preceding the → tone or tonic syllable, or the vowel that immediately precedes the tonic syllable.

**PRIESTLY SOURCE.** → JEDP.

**PRIMARY TENSES.** In Greek the → present, → future, → perfect, and → future perfect → tenses of the → indicative mood; they share common → affixes that relate to present and future time. → Secondary Tenses.

**PRIMITIVE GOSPEL.** → Urevangelium.

**PRIMITIVE MARK.** → Urmarkus.

**PRINCIPAL CLAUSE.** Another name for → main clause.

**PRINCIPAL PARTS.** The basic → stems of a verb one must know in order to construct the remaining forms of its → conjugation. In Hebrew, the principal parts are the → qal, → piel, → hiphil, → niphal, and → hithpael; in Greek, the present, future, aorist, perfect, perfect middle, and aorist passive.

**PRIVATIVE.** In Hebrew, the preposition *min* used in the sense of "away from," "without"; it signifies privation, negation, or the absence of something. *Heb:* "*away* *from* the dew of heaven above" (Gen. 27:39). The Greek *alpha* privative is a → prefix with negative force. *Gk: pistos,* "believing"; *apistos,* "unbelieving" (Luke 9:41).

**PROCLISIS/PROCLITIC.** Certain words that stand in a syntactically conjunctive relationship in Hebrew and are joined by the → maqqeph; most frequently occurs with monosyllabic words. In Greek, monosyllabics so closely linked to a following word as to have no separate accent. *Heb: min ʾiš. Gk: hoi anthrōpoi.*

**PROCLITIC MEM.** In Hebrew, a *mem* that is written at the beginning of a word and as part of it. *Heb: miḏbār,* desert."

**PRODIORTHOSIS.** A rhetorical figure in which an anticipatory correction is made of a statement that is likely to offend. *Gk:* "I hope you will put up with a little of my foolishness" (2 Cor. 11:1).

**PROEM.** Greek for "prelude." A shorter prefatory section or preliminary comment; the literary equivalent of an overture. In rabbinic → homilies, the introduction of a key OT text, a pattern also found in the NT. *Gk:* Abraham the example of justification by faith, based on Gen. 15:6 (Rom. 4:1–25).

**PROFILE METHOD.** In NT → textual criticism, a sampling procedure that uses selected readings to isolate characteristic profiles and thereby distinguish groups of → manuscripts. Based on the quantitative method of Colwell and Tune. → Genealogical Method.

**PROGRESSIVE.** → Linear.

**PROGRESSIVE ASSIMILATION.** → Assimilation.

**PROJECTING PARALLELISM.** Another name for → synthetic parallelism.

**PROLEGOMENON (pl., PROLEGOMENA).** An introduction

to or preliminary remarks for a study. *Ex:* Julius Wellhausen, *Prolegomena to the History of Ancient Israel.*

**PROLEPSIS.** In grammar, the transfer of a word to the → main clause in anticipation of, or in order to denote, the result of the action of the verb (e.g., to shoot a person *dead*). Especially, the anticipation of the subject of the → subordinate clause by making it the object of the main clause. *Heb:* Gen. 1:4a; Neh. 9:15b; Dan. 4:6a. *Gk:* Luke 19:3; Mark 1:24; Rev. 3:9. In chronology, it refers to an error by which a date earlier than the correct date is assigned to an event, or a prophetic technique treating a future event as past (e.g., Amos 5:1–2). → Prophetic Perfect.

**PROLOGUE.** The opening section of a literary work, generally essential to the meaning and structure, as opposed to a preface. *Heb:* the prologue of Job (Job 1:1–2:13). *Gk:* the prologue of John (John 1:1–18).

**PRONOMINAL.** A term used by some grammarians for → pronoun, or that which is related to the pronoun. In Hebrew, pronominal → suffixes can be added to verbs, nouns, and → particles.

**PRONOUN.** A word that is used to take the place of a noun. Frequently used pronouns are *I, he, she, me, who, this.*

**PRONOUNCEMENT STORY.** A phrase coined by Vincent Taylor to be a conservative alternative to the use of → paradigm and → apothegm in German → form criticism. The term maintains a heightened appreciation for the historicity of both Jesus' sayings and their narrative settings.

**PROPAROXYTONE.** In Greek, a word with acute → accent on the → antepenult. There is no equivalent of this accent in Hebrew, as the principal accent will be either on the last or next to last syllable. › Milʿel, → Milraʿ.

**PROPERISPOMENON.** In Greek, a word with the circumflex accent on the → penult.

**PROPER NOUN.** → Noun.

**PROPHETIC PERFECT.** The writer or speaker is so certain that an event will take place in the future that he speaks of it as though it already had taken place by using the → perfect form of the Hebrew verb; it is also called the *perfect of certainty. Heb:* "Fallen is Virgin Israel" (Amos 5:2). → Prolepsis.

**PROPHETS.** A class of people in OT times who received messages from God and transmitted them to the people. Also, the name of the third division of the Hebrew Bible. → Nebiim.

**PROSE.** The ordinary form of written or spoken language. It does not make use of the special literary forms of structure, → meter, and rhythm that are characteristic of poetry.

**PROSELYTE.** A convert to a religious faith; in NT times it was used especially of a convert to Judaism.

**PROSTAXIS.** The linking together of several coordinate clauses by use of particles such as "and." These particles frequently function more like periods than conjunctions. In Hebrew, the initial *waw,* "and," frequently does not link the clause to the previous clause. *Heb:* "They said to me" (Exod. 32:23), lit., "*And* they said to me"). *Gk: kai* and *de* perform this function in Greek; cf. Matt. 1:2–16.

**PROSTHETIC ALEPH.** In Hebrew, an *aleph* with its vowel is prefixed to some words to avoid harshness in the pronunciation. *Heb:* 'ezrōî, "my arm" (Job 31:22). Also called *aleph prostheticum.*

**PROTASIS.** The → subordinate or "if" clause that expresses the condition in a → conditional sentence (→ apodosis). *Heb:* "If you fully obey the LORD . . . [protasis], the LORD your God will set you high above all the nations on earth [apodosis]" (Deut. 28:1). *Gk:* "If you love me [protasis], you will obey what I command [apodosis]" (John 14:15).

**PROTEVANGELIUM.** Greek, "first gospel." This term refers to Gen. 3:15, which is interpreted by many as a reference to Christ's victory over Satan, and therefore as the first statement of the gospel in the Bible.

**PROTHESIS.** In liturgy, prothesis refers to the preparation and preliminary oblation of bread and wine before its ceremonial use, to the altar or table, or to the chapel where it is done.

**PROTHETIC VOWEL.** Literally, "set before," "set in front of." A short vowel prefixed to certain stems in → Koine Greek. → Aphaeresis.

**PROTO-LUCIAN.** A revision of the → Old Greek in the second or first century b.c., to bring it into agreement with the Palestinian Hebrew text.

**PROTO-LUKE.** A hypothetical document composed of → Q and → L (minus the birth narratives), suggested by B. H. Streeter to account for the so-called "great omission" and block structure of Luke when placed beside Mark. In this view, → canonical Luke is a revision of Proto-Luke made with the insertion of Marcan material.

**PROTO-LXX.** Another name for → Old Greek.

**PROTO-MASORETIC TEXT.** A term used by some scholars for the Hebrew text forms earlier than the → Ben Asher text, particularly the text current among the sectaries of Qumran. Also called pre-Masoretic.

**PROTO-THEODOTION.** Another name for the → Kaige recension.

**PSALTER.** Another name for the Book of Psalms.

**PSEUDEPIGRAPHA.** The name given to a large body of Jewish writings that were not included in the OT → canon or in the → Apocrypha. These books were written ca. 200 B.C.–A.D. 100.

**PSEUDONYM/PSEUDONYMOUS.** A fictitious name or a name of a well-known person from the past assumed by a writer who for various reasons prefers not to use his own name. *Ex:* The Wisdom of Solomon in the → Apocrypha; many scholars classify the books of Daniel and 2 Peter as pseudonymous; many of the → Pseudepigrapha, including the Paralipomena of Jeremiah and the Apocalypse of Moses.

**PSILOSIS.** The tendency toward de-aspiration in Greek pronunciation during the → Hellenistic period, i.e., decrease in the use of the *h* sound or rough breathing. → Aspiration, → Breathing Marks.

**PUAL.** A verbal form in Hebrew that expresses intensive or emphatic action and passive → voice. *Heb:* "There was Baal's altar, *demolished*" (Judg. 6:28).

**PUNCTA EXTRAORDINARIA.** Fifteen occurrences of dots over single letters or whole words in the → Masoretic text; they indicate some kind of textual or doctrinal question of the scribes concerning the traditional text, which, however, they did not dare alter. Ernest Würthwein, *The Text of the Old Testament*, 2nd ed., p. 17, lists all examples of puncta extraordinaria found in the OT. Also called special points. → Diacritical Marks.

**PUNCTILIAR.** An → aspect of the verb that depicts the action as a "point" (as opposed to → linear) or reflects an undefined, summary point of view; a basic force of the → aorist tense. *Ex:* "I walk" in contrast to "I am walking."

**PURPOSE.** Another name for → telic.

**PURPOSE CLAUSE.** A type of → adverbial clause that answers the question "for what end or purpose?"; introduced in English by "in order to," or "so that." Also called → *telic* or *final clause.*

**Q.** → Siglum for the Synoptic sayings-source or the → double tradition of Matthew and Luke; derived from the German word *Quelle*, "source." Used in → source-critical research of nineteenth-century German scholarship. There is no agreement on the question whether Q was written or oral or on its origin, date, and contents. Although currently disputed, a source like Q remains integral to the → two source hypothesis.

**QAL.** A verbal form in Hebrew that expresses simple action and active → voice; it is sometimes spelled Kal. *Ex:* "Then Jacob *gave* Esau some bread and some lentil stew" (Gen. 25:34).

**QAL WAHOMER.** The first of Hillel's seven → middot, the inference from the lesser to the greater: "if such be true, how much more. . . ." Equivalent to the argument → a fortiori or → a minore ad majus.

**QERE.** → Kethib.

**QERE PERPETUUM.** Some very common words that are always read other than according to the → kethib; in these cases it was not considered necessary to write the → qere in the margin, but its vowels were written as part of the word in the text. *Heb: Hiw'*, wherever *hiw'* stands for the feminine pronoun *hî'*, "she."

**QINAH.** In Hebrew poetry, the name of a lament or dirge →
meter characterized by three accents to one line and
two accents to the second line (frequently written 3:2).
*Heb:* Much of the Book of Lamentations is characterized by qinah meter.

**QOHELETH.** The Hebrew name of the Book of Ecclesiastes
(also spelled Koheleth); its meaning is uncertain.

**QUARTO.** In printing, a sheet of paper folded twice and cut
to produce four leaves, or the size of a book made of
sheets folded twice; the result is eight pages to a sheet.
Abbreviated 4to or 4°. → Folio, → Octavo.

**QUATERNION.** Four sheets of papyrus or parchment folded
together to make eight leaves or sixteen pages, forming
a section (→ quire) of a → codex.

**QUATRAIN.** In poetry, a stanza of four lines.

**QUELLE.** → Q.

**QUIESCENT LETTERS.** In Hebrew, the letters *aleph, he,
waw,* and *yod* are so weak in pronunciation that under
certain conditions they lose their consonantal character and quiesce (that is, become silent). *Heb: lîhûḏāh,*
"to Judah," *lē'lōhîm,* "to God."

**QUINTA.** Fifth Greek version (in addition to Aquila, Symmachus, Theodotion, and the LXX), used for some
books in Origen's → *Hexapla.* → Sexta, → Septima.

**QUIRE.** Section of a → codex, made from several sheets
folded together and stitched. A four-sheet quire is called
a → *quaternion.*

**R.** A biblical → redactor.

**RABBI.** The transliteration of Hebrew *rabbî*, "my master" or "my teacher." Originally a respectful term of address used in greeting experts in the law, it became a title in the first century A.D. for a member of the → Tannaim. *Gk:* used in the Gospels as an honorary designation of Jesus (e.g., Mark 9:5; John 1:38; 6:25), also in its Palestinian → Aramaic form, *rabbonî* (Mark 10:51; John 20:16).

**RADICAL.** That belonging to the root of a word, e.g., a primitive form that equals the root. In Hebrew, another name for a basic → root letter (or → consonant) of a word.

**RAS SHAMRA TABLETS.** The name of a collection of texts from ancient Ugarit that have revealed a great deal about the religious, literary, historical, and political situation in Canaan around 1400 B.C. → Ugaritic.

**RATIONAL CRITICISM.** Another name for → eclecticism.

**READING.** The form or version of a given word or passage in a particular text or → manuscript. → Variant Reading.

**RECEIVED TEXT.** Another name for → textus receptus.

**RECENSION.** An edition of an ancient text that involves a revision of an earlier text form.

**RECEPTOR.** One who receives a message or text. → Receptor Language.

**RECEPTOR LANGUAGE.** The language into which a translation is made by the → receptor. In a translation from Greek to English, Greek is the → source language, English the receptor language. Also called *target language.*

**RECITATIVUM.** The use of the conjunction *that* to introduce a direct quotation, the equivalent of quotation marks in English; in Hebrew, *kî,* in Greek, *hoti. Heb:* "The Lord answered, [*kî*] 'I will be with you'" (Judg. 6:16). *Gk:* "A man with leprosy . . . begged him on his knees, [*hoti*] 'If you are willing, you can make me clean'" (Mark 1:40).

**RECOMMENDATION.** → Commendation.

**RECTO.** The front of a → papyrus sheet where the strips run horizontally, as opposed to → verso; the inside of a → scroll (usually a scroll was written on the front side only). The right-hand page in a → codex and in our books.

**REDACTION.** → Redactor.

**REDACTION CRITICISM.** A study of how the Scriptures reached their final form from the earliest oral form, through a process of editing and composition, to their written form. Especially in the Gospels, the study of the editorial techniques and contributions of the gospel writers. Also called → *composition criticism.*

**REDACTOR.** One who edited a document at a later time to bring it up to date or who in some other way modified a text. He frequently collected and edited older and smaller units of material into newer, larger ones. The process of editing is called *redaction. Ex:* Mark as redactor of the earliest gospel tradition.

**REDAKTIONSGESCHICHTE.** The German term for → redaction criticism.

**REDEMPTIVE HISTORY.** Translation of the German term → Heilsgeschichte.

**REDUNDANCY/REDUNDANT.** A general term that means wordiness or the use of unnecessary words. *Ex:* a widow *woman.* → Pleonasm, → Tautology.

**REDUPLICATION.** The repetition of the initial sound of a Greek word; when used to form the → perfect tense, initial vowels are lengthened, while initial consonants are doubled with *e* inserted to make a new syllable.

**REFERENTIAL MEANING.** Another term for → denotative meaning.

**REFLEXIVE PRONOUN.** A → pronoun used as an object, referring back to the subject of the verb. *Ex:* "I dress *myself.*"

**REFLEXIVE VOICE.** Denotes an action that is directed back upon the agent or subject; expressed in Hebrew by the → niphal and the → hithpael, in Greek by the → middle voice. *Heb:* "I have . . . *kept myself* from sin" (Ps. 18:23). *Gk:* "Then he went away and *hanged himself*" (Matt. 27:5).

**REGIMEN.** → Nomen Regens.

**REGRESSIVE ASSIMILATION.** → Assimilation.

**REGULA FIDEI.** Latin for "rule of faith." The extension of the → kerygma to creedal-type confessions used for → catechesis and as criteria of orthodoxy in the early church.

**REL./RELL.** Abbreviations of Latin *reliqui,* "remaining." Used in a → critical apparatus to mean "the remaining manuscripts read . . ."

**RELATIVE CLAUSE.** Primarily, an adjectival, → subordinate clause, introduced by a relative pronoun, that describes the → antecedent of the pronoun. *Heb:* "You and Aaron are to number . . . all the men . . . *who are able to serve in the army*" (Num. 1:3). *Gk:* "to abstain from sinful desires, *which war against your soul*" (1 Peter 2:11).

**RELIGIO-HISTORICAL CRITICISM.** The comparative study of the religions of the ancient Near East. It is also called the *history of religion* or → *comparative religion*. → History of Religions School.

**RELIGIONSGESCHICHTLICHE SCHULE.** The German term for the → History of Religions School.

**RENDER.** A synonym for "translate." *Ex:* We render Hebrew and Greek into English.

**REPETITIVE PARALLELISM.** Another name for → climactic parallelism.

**RESTRICTIVE.** A restrictive → phrase or → clause is one that is essential, i.e., it could not be omitted without changing the meaning of the main clause. *Heb:* "the Xerxes *who ruled over 127 provinces*" (Esth. 1:1). *Gk:* "When Jesus saw . . . the disciple *whom he loved* standing nearby" (John 19:26). → Nonrestrictive.

**RESULTATIVE.** An → aspect of the verb that indicates the completion or result of the action; sometimes used as the equivalent of effective, → culminative, → perfective, or → consummative. → Effective Aorist.

**RESULT CLAUSE.** A type of → adverbial clause that answers the question, "what happened as a result?"; introduced in English by "that" or "so that." *Heb:* "God is not a man, *that* he should lie" (Num. 23:19). *Gk:* "For God so loved the world *that* he gave his one and only son" (John 3:16). Also called *consecutive* or *ecbatic clause.*

**RESUMPTIVE.** A term used for the introduction of an → apodosis.

**RETAINED OBJECT.** Active verbs that take two objects (→ factitive) retain the remote or impersonal object in the passive voice, while the other becomes the subject. *Ex:* active voice, "I will show *you* the *land*"; passive voice, "*you* will be shown the *land*"; cf. Gen. 12:1; Exod. 25:40; Luke 12:47; Gal. 2:7.

**RETROVERSION.** Translation of the Greek text back into the Hebrew on which it was allegedly based. Attempts have been made by the use of retroversion to show that some NT books were originally written in Hebrew rather than in Greek.

**RHETORIC.** The art of expressive speech or discourse, used especially of literary composition; skillful or artistic use of speech.

**RHETORICAL CRITICISM.** A study of the structural patterns of a literary unit with attention given to various devices (such as → parallelism, → chiasmus, etc.) used in its composition. It gives special attention to the unique stylistic characteristics of the writer or speaker.

**RHETORICAL QUESTION.** An expression cast in the form of a question, not to elicit an answer but to make a stylistic point of emphasis. The expected answer is understood. A rhetorical question may be asked to introduce a subject which the speaker or writer wishes to discuss. *Heb:* " 'Does Job fear God for nothing?' Satan replied" (Job 1:9). *Gk:* "How shall we escape if we ignore such a great salvation?" (Heb. 2:3).

**RÎB PATTERN.** A form of prophetic speech characterized by its similarities to a lawsuit. It may include a summons to the offending party by the one making the complaint, a reminder of past favors given to the offender, specific accusations, and a call to witnesses to verify the charges. *Heb:* Mic. 6:1–16.

**ROOT.** That part of a word left when all → affixes are removed; the → morpheme that carries the minimal unit of meaning in a word and can be common to several different words. The three consonants in Hebrew that ordinarily compose the basic uninflected spelling of a word are called the *root letters*. Occasionally a Hebrew word may have two or four root letters. *Gk:* the root *dik* is common to *dikaios*, "righteous," *dikē*, "justice," and *dikaioō*, "to acquit." → Lexeme.

**ROOT VERB.** Another name for a → strong verb.

**ROUGH BREATHING.** → Breathing Marks.

**RSV.** Abbreviation for the *Revised Standard Version*, a revision of the → RV and → ASV in the light of the → KJV and not a completely new translation; it was first published in its entirety in 1952.

**RV.** Abbreviation for the *Revised Version*, a British revision of the → KJV; it was first published in its entirety in 1885.

**SACHKRITIK.** German for "subject criticism." A hermeneutical principle employed by Rudolf Bultmann and his school to distinguish theological → exegesis from → historical criticism; the subject matter is made applicable even when the language describing it is deemed inappropriate. Interpretation of the text hinges on what the author is taken to mean, not primarily on what he says.

**SACRED HISTORY.** Translation of the German term → Heilsgeschichte.

**SAGA.** A common → narrative → genre in the OT; it is a story that contains fundamental truths apart from historical consideration; it usually actualizes the event vividly. *Ex:* the story of Sodom in Genesis 19 is classified as a saga.

**SALVATION HISTORY.** Translation of the German term → Heilsgeschichte.

**SAMARITAN PENTATEUCH.** A Hebrew → recension of the → Pentateuch, retained and used in the Samaritan community during the → Second Temple period; a → pre-Masoretic textual tradition that was probably revised in the first century B.C. It differs significantly from the → Masoretic text but preserves ancient and important readings.

**SAPIENTIAL.** From Latin *sapientia*, "wisdom." Having to do with → wisdom and → wisdom literature.

**SATIRE.** Prose or poetry in which contemporary vices or follies are held up to ridicule; its popular adaptation in Horace and Juvenal is full of invective and sarcasm. *Ex:* Paul's satirical outburst against the intruders in the church at Corinth (2 Cor. 10–13).

**SC., SCIL.** Abbreviations of Latin *scilicet*, "one may know." Used in quotations in the sense of "to wit," "namely," to clarify the meaning of the original.

**SCHEMA ATTICUM.** The classical Greek rule of → concord, which states that a neuter plural subject takes a singular verb; the NT observes the rule, particularly with → abstract nouns. *Gk:* "These are [lit., is] the names of the twelve apostles" (Matt. 10:2).

**SCHEMA ETYMOLOGICUM.** Another name for → cognate accusative.

**SCHOLION (pl., SCHOLIA).** Notes in the margins of ancient → manuscripts that record comments on the language, grammar, and subject matter of the text; often derived from older commentaries. See also → hyponema.

**SCIL.** → SC.

**SCRIBAL ERROR.** An obvious mistake made by a → scribe in the copying of a document. → Dittography, → Haplography, → Homoioarchton, → Homoioteleuton.

**SCRIBAL GLOSS.** Additions to the text made by a → scribe while copying the text, either for the purpose of clarification or for correction. → Gloss.

**SCRIBE.** Originally a secular office held by one who was skilled in the art of writing. In postexilic Judaism the scribes composed a class of professional interpreters and teachers of the Law. → Sopher, → Amanuensis.

**SCRIPTIO CONTINUA.** A Latin term for writing without any spaces between words and sentences; a characteristic of Greek → manuscripts, but not of Hebrew.

**SCRIPTIO DEFECTIVA.** Latin for → defective writing.

**SCRIPTIO PLENA.** Latin for → plena writing.

· **SCROLL.** → Papyrus, → parchment, or leather sheets joined together in rolls, usually 10–12 inches wide and up to 35 feet long. Writing was usually on one side only in vertical columns a few inches wide. The scrolls were read by rolling from left to right between two rollers. → Codex.

**SEBIR (pl., SEBIRIN).** In the Hebrew text, where a word appears in an unusual form or with an unusual meaning, the normal form or word that would be expected is placed in the margin and introduced by $s^e b\hat{\imath}r$ (the passive participle of "suppose") as a warning to copyists to avoid changing the accepted text in favor of a reading that seems preferable. *Heb:* Gen. 19:8, 49:13.

**SEC.** Abbreviation of Latin *secundum*, "according to." Used in → textual criticism to cite a → manuscript.

**SECONDARY TENSES.** In Greek, the → imperfect, → aorist, and → pluperfect of the → indicative mood; they share common → affixes that relate to past time. → Primary Tenses.

**SECOND SOPHISTIC.** A movement of itinerant teachers and practitioners of Greek → rhetoric in the early Roman empire; literary → Atticism and the revival of classical oratory in the writings of Dio Chrysostom, Herodes Atticus, Aelius Aristides, Flavius Philostratus, and Lucian. → Epideictic Oratory.

**SECOND TEMPLE PERIOD.** A designation of the Hellenistic-Roman period from the viewpoint of the Jewish commonwealth, beginning with the subjugation of Palestine by Alexander in 332 B.C. and extending through the first Jewish revolt to the destruction of the Temple in A.D. 70.

**SEDER (pl., SEDARIM).** The sections of Scripture into which Palestinian Jews divided the → Torah, to be read weekly in worship services over a three-year period. The beginning of a seder is indicated in the margin in → BHS; see also → parash. The word is also used to designate the ceremony observed on Passover night and the six major divisions of the → Mishnah and → Talmud.

**SEGHOLATE.** In Hebrew, a term used of words that are characterized by the use of *e* vowels in spelling; these are sometimes called *second declension nouns. Heb: nepeš, 'emet, ṣedeq,* etc.

**SEMANTICS.** The science of the meaning of words. In biblical studies, especially the view that word meaning is not simply a listing of independent items but a study of fields wherein words interrelate and define each other.

**SEMITE/SEMITIC.** A descendant of Shem, the son of Noah (Gen. 10:21–31). Included Babylonians, Assyrians, and Arameans in ancient times, as well as Arabs and Jews.

**SEMITISM.** A word or construction derived from Hebrew or Aramaic, more specifically those features of the → LXX and the Greek NT that reflect the influence of Hebrew (→ Hebraism) or Aramaic (→ Aramaism).

**SEMIVOWEL.** A sound that functions as a consonant but also has the phonetic quality of a short vowel. In Greek, the semivowels are *iota* and *upsilon.* → Half Vowel.

**SENSUS PLENIOR.** Latin for the "fuller meaning" of a passage of Scripture intended by God but not clearly intended by the human author or understood by the original hearers or readers.

**SENTENCE.** According to traditional definition, a grammatical unit containing an independent verb (→ main clause) or expressing a complete thought.

**SEPHARDIC.** A pronunciation of the Hebrew language characteristic of the Sephardim, the Jews in Spain and Portugal; it is the pronunciation used in modern Israel. → Ashkenazic.

**SEPTIMA.** A seventh Greek version used for some books in Origen's → Hexapla. → Quinta, → Sexta.

**SEPTUAGINT.** From Latin *septuaginta*, "seventy." Greek translation of the OT that (according to the *Letter of Aristeas*) was made by Jews of Alexandria, Egypt, around 250 B.C.; the word is frequently written as → LXX. Strictly speaking, the term should apply only to the → Pentateuch, but the name came to be used of the entire Greek translation of the OT.

**SEPTUAGINTISM.** A word or idiom in the Greek NT that is due to the influence of the → Septuagint; because of the influence of Hebrew on the Septuagint, many Septuagintisms are properly → Semitisms. *Gk:* the use of *tou* with the infinitive after verbs (Luke 4:10; 9:51; Acts 3:12; 15:20).

**SEQ.** Abbreviation of Latin *sequens*, "following." Used in → textual criticism to indicate the following verses, chapters, or sections.

**SERVANT SONGS.** The designation of Isa. 42:1–4; 49:1–6; 50:4–9; 52:13–53:12 because these passages describe one who is a servant of the Lord. The designation was first proposed by Bernard Duhm in 1892.

**SETUMA.** In the Hebrew Bible, a closed paragraph, indicated by a *samek* in the gap in the text. → Pethuca.

**SEXTA.** A sixth Greek version used for some books in Origen's → Hexapla. → Quinta, → Septima.

**SHADDAI, SHADDAY.** One of the Hebrew names for God, usually translated as "Almighty." Frequently combined with → El. *Heb:* Gen. 28:3.

**SHALOM.** Hebrew for "peace." The word should be understood in a much broader sense than our word "peace" as "wholeness," "completeness," or "wellbeing."

**SHARPENING.** A closed syllable in Hebrew whose final consonant is doubled is called sharpened. *Heb: hammā-'ôr.* Certain vowels may also be sharpened; ordinarily, but not always, this occurs when a short vowel is made into a long vowel. *Heb: 'āreṣ* for *'ereṣ* when an article is prefixed; *seghol* may be sharpened to *hireq* and *qames* to *qibbus.*

**SHEKINAH.** From Hebrew, "to dwell." A way of referring to the divine presence of God that developed during the → Intertestamental period. The word is not found in the Bible but is found in the → Targums and rabbinic writings.

**SHEMA.** The title given to Deut. 6:4–9, Judaism's confession of faith, proclaiming the unity of God; it is taken from the first word of the passage, "Hear."

**SHEMONEH ESREH.** The Hebrew name for the → Eighteen Benedictions.

**SHEWA.** Another name for a → half vowel.

**SIBILANTS.** The consonants that are characterized by the *s* sound. In Hebrew, the sibilants are *zayin, samek, ṣade, śin, šin;* in Greek, *sigma.* Sometimes called → *spirants.*

**SIGLUM (pl., SIGLA).** A letter (or letters), abbreviation, or symbol used to indicate a → manuscript or source of an edited text. *Ex:* 1QpHab for the → *pesher* commentary on Habakkuk from Qumran cave 1 (→ *Dead Sea*

*Scrolls*); → Q for the common tradition of Matthew and Luke.

**SILLUQ.** → Pause.

**SIMILE.** An explicit comparison (usually with the word "like") of two things that in their general nature are different from each other; cf. → metaphor, which is an implied comparison. *Heb:* "I am *like* a moth to Ephraim" (Hos. 5:12); *Gk:* "They are *like* children sitting in the marketplace" (Luke 7:32).

**SIMILITUDE.** A → parable form proper, a figurative story that compares an unknown reality (the kingdom of God in Jesus' use) to a known image, a typical circumstance, or event. The image depicts things that happen every day and general situations accessible to everyone. *Ex:* the parables of the lost sheep and the lost coin (Luke 15:4–10).

**SIMPLE WAW.** Another name for → *waw* conjunctive.

**SITZ IM LEBEN.** A German expression used in → form criticism to describe the "situation in life," i.e., the cultural context out of which a certain form of literary expression arose, especially the community setting in which a form was developed and understood.

**SMOOTH BREATHING.** → Breathing Marks.

**SOLECISM.** An impropriety or irregularity in grammar, from Soloi (or Soli), a city of ancient Cilicia, where a substandard form of Greek was spoken. Solecisms are prominent in the Book of Revelation, usually a lapse of → concord. *Gk:* masculine for feminine gender (Rev. 11:4; 14:19; 17:3), nominative for genitive case (Rev. 2:13; 3:12; 7:4; 8:9; 14:12).

**SONANTS.** The → liquids and → nasals that can form syllables by themselves; especially after the loss of a preceding vowel, they function as vowel sounds; also called →

*vocalic.* In Hebrew, the sonants are *yod, lamed, mem, nun,* and *resh;* in Greek, *lambda, mu, nu,* and *rho.*

**SOPHER (pl., SOPHERIM).** Hebrew word for → scribe. The sopherim were teachers of the OT and guardians of its text.

**SORITES.** A chain of propositions in which the predicate of each link is the subject of the next; the conclusion is formed in circular fashion by the first subject. See also → climax. *Gk:* "hope . . . suffering, suffering . . . perseverance, perseverance . . . character, and character . . . hope" (Rom. 5:2b–5a; cf. 8:29–30; 10:13–15).

**SOURCE CRITICISM.** A special aspect of → literary criticism, an analytical → methodology used in the study of biblical books to discover individual documents (or sources) that were used in the construction of a particular literary unit as we now have it. *Ex:* the source hypotheses postulated for the → Synoptic problem.

**SOURCE LANGUAGE.** The language in which the message or text was originally produced. In a translation from Hebrew to English, English is the → receptor language, Hebrew the source language.

**SPECIAL POINTS.** → Puncta Extraordinaria.

**SPIRANT/SPIRANTIZATION.** A consonant uttered with a decided friction and continuation of the breath against some part of the oral passage (as *f, s, sh*); also called *continuants.* The term is also used to describe the softer sound given in Hebrew to the → begad kephat letters, i.e., their pronunciation without the → daghesh lene. → Aspiration, → Fricative.

**SPIRITUS ASPER.** Latin term for rough breathing. → Breathing Marks.

**SPIRITUS LENIS.** Latin term for smooth breathing. → Breathing Marks.

**SPURIOUS DIPHTHONG.** → Improper Diphthong.

**STAIRLIKE PARALLELISM.** Another name for → climactic parallelism.

**STANZA.** A unit or division of a poem consisting of a group of two or more of lines; also called a *strophe*.

**STATIVE VERB, STATIC VERB.** A stative verb is one that indicates a state of being or relationship rather than action. In Hebrew, its vowel pattern is different from that of verbs of action or motion. Greek statives include *eimi, ginomai,* and *huparchō. Heb:* "the hands . . . will be strengthened (2 Sam. 16:21). *Gk:* "Who, *being* in very nature God" (Phil. 2:6).

**STELE.** A slab or pillar of stone on which inscriptions were made in ancient times. One of the best known is the Mesha Stele (also called the Moabite Stone), which describes the Moabite revolt against Israel that is also found in 2 Kings 3.

**STEM.** The noun or verb base formed by the addition of derivational → affixes to the → root. Thus, in Greek, *dōro-* is the stem of the noun *dōron,* "gift"; *dō* is the root, *ro* is the affix (in this case, a → suffix) Also called *base* in recent grammars. In Hebrew, the term is used to designate verb forms that express certain kinds of action and voice; the major Hebrew verbal stems are → qal, → niphal, → piel, → pual, → hithpael, → hiphil, and → hophal.

**STEMMA CODICUM.** A genealogical chart of the descent of → manuscripts, showing the history of transmission of a text in its various → recensions.

**STICH, STICHOS.** A single line of prose or poetry; also called → *colon* or *line.* The term is sometimes used to designate each of the two parts that normally constitute a line of Hebrew poetry. → Stichometry.

**STICHOMETRY.** The ancient method of book measurement; a → manuscript was measured by the number of → stichs it contained, and the → scribe was paid accordingly. The Greek stich averaged sixteen syllables or thirty-six letters. Early NT manuscripts have stichometric notations. *Ex:* Papyrus 46 notes 316 stichs for Ephesians.

**STOPS.** Another name for → mutes.

**STRONG VERB.** In Hebrew, the regular verb whose → stem consonants do not change, i.e., remain unmodified in → conjugation, in contrast to the → weak verb. In Greek, a → tense stem formed from the verb stem or root itself by → vowel gradation.

**STRONG WAW.** Another name for → *waw* consecutive.

**STROPHE.** Another designation for → stanza.

**STRUCTURAL ANALYSIS, STRUCTURAL CRITICISM, STRUCTURALISM.** A study of the structure of the language to which the biblical texts conform in order to be intelligible; often concerned primarily with the sentence and smaller units. It has also been called → *stylistic criticism.* In a wider sense, it examines the structural features of biblical narratives that can be analyzed in terms of underlying modes of expression inherent to all human thought. Interest in the author's purpose and historical dimensions of the text are minimal.

**STYLISTIC CRITICISM.** A study of verse structure and literary patterns; the term is used interchangeably with → structural analysis.

**SUBAPOSTOLIC AGE.** Another term for → postapostolic age.

**SUBJECT.** The → substantive most closely related to the verb in a sentence; that which can have a → predicate.

Subject and verb together constitute the core of a sentence. *Heb:* "*Pharaoh* had a dream" (Gen. 41:1). *Gk:* "*Jesus* stepped into a boat" (Matt. 9:1).

**SUBJECT COMPLEMENT.** A word or phrase, used with a → copula, that completes the meaning of the subject. A noun renames the subject: "He is *John*," an adjective describes the subject: "He is *tall.*" Also called *predicate nominative, predicate noun,* or *predicate adjective. Heb:* "Your name is *Jacob*" (Gen. 35:10). *Gk:* "Salt is *good*" (Mark 9:50).

**SUBJECTIVE GENITIVE.** The genitive (noun or possessive pronoun) is the subject of the relationship expressed. *Heb:* "visions of God" = "visions given by (belonging to) God" (Ezek. 1:1); *Gk:* "work of faith" = "work produced by faith" (1 Thess. 1:3). → Objective Genitive.

**SUBJUNCTIVE MOOD.** A → mood of probability that expresses wish, purpose, supposition, or condition; it may express a hypothetical situation. *Heb:* "If I shut up heaven that there is no rain" (2 Chron. 7:13 KJV). *Gk:* "all this I have told you so that you will not go astray" (John 16:1).

**SUBORDINATE/SUBORDINATION.** The linking of grammatical units of unequal rank, making one dependent on the other; also called → *hypotaxis.*

**SUBORDINATE CLAUSE.** A clause that is dependent on another clause for its meaning; it does not make sense when standing alone. It is usually introduced by a → particle, → conjunction, or → adverb and can be a part of a → main clause or a → complex sentence. Also called *dependent clause. Heb:* "because of the evil you have done" (Jer. 4:4) *Gk:* "because of their lack of faith" (Matt. 13:58).

**SUBSTANTIVE.** Any part of speech that is used as a noun equivalent. *Ex:* an → adjective, → participle, or → infinitive used as the subject of a sentence, e.g., "*to err* is human."

**SUCCESSION NARRATIVE.** A term coined by Leonhard Rost in 1926 to designate 2 Sam. 9–20 and 1 Kings 1–2; the term is used by many scholars in recognition of the unity of this block of historical → narrative material.

**SUFFIX.** One or more syllables added to the end of a → root or to a → stem in Hebrew and Greek that will modify its meaning. Also called an *afformative* or *sufformative. Heb:* → pronominal suffixes added to the noun to indicate → person, → gender, and → number. *Gk:* suffix *thē* to form the aorist passive.

**SUFFORMATIVE.** Another name for → suffix.

**SUMMARY AORIST.** Another name for the → constative aorist.

**SUPERLATIVE DEGREE.** Forms of adjectives and adverbs, or adjectival and adverbial constructions, that express unsurpassed extent of quality, quantity, or intensity. In English, the superlative degree is expressed by an adjective with the suffix *-est* (rich*est*) or "most" with an adverb (*most* richly). In Hebrew, it is expressed by various means other than suffixes (e.g., repetition of words); in Greek, by the use of certain particles and suffixes. *Heb:* "Holy of Holies" = "Most Holy Place" (1 Kings 6:16). *Gk:* "according to the *strictest* sect of our religion, I lived as a Pharisee" (Acts 26:5). → Comparative Degree, → Elative.

**SUPPLETION.** The supplying of an unrelated → stem to fill out a → conjugation or → declension. → Defective Verb.

**SUSPENDED CASE.** → Casus Pendens.

**S.V.** Abbreviation of Latin *sub voce* "under the voice [i.e., utterance]" or *sub verbo,* "under the word." It means "look up the reference under the entry or heading named." Equivalent to the arrow (→) in this dictionary.

**SYLLABARY.** A list of syllables; a set or table of signs denoting syllables; a dictionary for an ancient syllabically-written language.

**SYLLABIC AUGMENT.** → Augment.

**SYLLABLE.** A unit of pronunciation in a word. As a general rule, a Hebrew syllable begins with one consonant followed by a vowel and may be closed by another consonant. A Hebrew word has as many syllables as → full vowels. A Greek word has as many syllables as vowels or diphthongs, divided on a pattern similar to English.

**SYLLEPSIS.** A rhetorical figure in which one word is applied to two others in different senses, e.g., "He looked with suspicion and a telescope." It is often confused with → zeugma; however, syllepsis requires only that the single word be understood in a different sense with each of the other two. *Gk:* "born of water and the Spirit" (John 3:5).

**SYMBIOSIS.** In biology, this term refers to the living together in intimate association or even close union of two dissimilar organisms. The term has been applied to tribal relationships.

**SYMMACHUS.** According to Eusebius, Symmachus was an Ebionite Christian who made a paraphrastic translation of the Hebrew OT into Greek in the second century A.D. His version depends upon Greek recensions and is extant only in the → Hexapla.

**SYMPLOCE.** The name given to the rhetorical device of combining → anaphora and → epiphora. *Heb:* Ps. 67. *Gk:* Rom. 8:24–25; 1 Cor. 1:27–28.

**SYNAESTHESIA.** A figure of speech in which two incongruous terms are linked metaphorically. *Heb:* "The words of Amos . . . what he saw" (Amos 1:1). *Gk:* "The god of this age has blinded the minds of unbelievers" (2 Cor. 4:4).

**SYNCHRONIC.** A term that refers to the static or fixed aspects of a language at a given point in time. *Heb:* Guttural letters do not take a → *daghesh forte* in Hebrew. *Gk:* The use of the perfect tense in first-century → Koine Greek. → Diachronic.

**SYNCOPE/SYNCOPATION.** The loss of one or more sounds or letters from the middle of a word, especially of a vowel before a vowel. *Heb: mûm* for *me'ûm; lammelek̲* for *le̲hammelek̲. Gk: nossos* for *neossos; esthōn* for *esthiōn.*

**SYNCRETISM.** The mingling of different religious beliefs through the influence of contact with other cultures. *Ex:* the fusion of traditional Greek cults and oriental beliefs in the → mystery religions; the blending of Yahweh worship with Baal worship in Israel.

**SYNECDOCHE.** A figure of speech in which a part represents the whole or the whole represents the part. *Heb:* "They have come under the protection of *my roof* [= my house]" (Gen. 19:8); *Gk:* "How beautiful are *the feet of those* [= messenger] who bring good news" (Rom. 10:15).

**SYNESIS.** Greek for "meaning." A grammatical construction made → ad sensum.

**SYNONYM.** A word that has approximately the same meaning and use as another, e.g., "purpose" is a synonym of "intention." *Heb: 'îš* and *geḇer* are synonyms for "man." *Gk:* the word "good" renders *agathos, kalos* (Matt. 7:18), and *chrēstos* (1 Cor. 15:33).

**SYNONYMOUS PARALLELISM.** In Hebrew poetry, the second line of a couplet repeats the thought of the first line in different words. *Ex:* Isa. 1:3.

**SYNOPSIS OF THE GOSPELS.** An edition of Matthew, Mark, and Luke (sometimes with John), arranged in parallel columns; the printed format preserves the full text of each Gospel in sequence. The first printed synopsis was made by J. J. Griesbach (1776). *Ex:* A. Huck and H. Greeven, *Synopse der drei ersten Evangelien;* K. Aland, *Synopsis of the Four Gospels.* → Harmony of the Gospels.

**SYNOPTIC GOSPELS.** From Greek *synoptikos,* "seen together." The first three Gospels (Matthew, Mark, and Luke), which present a parallel or common view of the story of Jesus. The term harks back to the printed → *Synopsis of the Gospels* by J. J. Griesbach (1776).

**SYNOPTIC PROBLEM, THE.** How to account for the similarities and differences in wording, content, and sequence among the → *Synoptic Gospels.* → Two Source Hypothesis, → Griesbach Hypothesis.

**SYNTAX.** A study of the arrangement of words to show their mutual relations in the sentence; sentence structures as opposed to → morphology, the study of word structure.

**SYNTHETIC PARALLELISM.** In Hebrew poetry, the second line of a couplet continues or advances the thought of the first. It is also called *formal, progressive, projecting,* or *expanded parallelism. Ex:* Prov. 4:23.

**SYRIAC LANGUAGE.** A member of the Semitic family of languages. It was similar to the → Aramaic dialect spoken in Palestine during the time of Jesus.

**SYRIAC VERSIONS.** Translations of the OT and NT into the → Syriac language. The oldest translation of the NT into Syriac, called the Old Syriac version, dates from the second century A.D. Related to it is Tatian's → *Diatessaron.* The principal Syriac version of the Bible is the → Peshitta, "the simple [version]."

**SYRIAN TEXT.** Another name for the → Byzantine text.

**SYZYGY.** In → Gnostic thought, a pair of cosmological opposites, such as male and female.

# T

**TALMUD.** The name given to the combination of the → Mishnah and the → Gemara; the compilations of rabbinic teaching and interpretation made by the → Amoraim during the third through sixth centuries A.D. in the academies of Babylonia and Palestine. These compilations are called the Babylonian Talmud, comprising some two and one-half million words, and the Palestinian or Jerusalem Talmud, a shorter version.

**TANAK.** Jewish name for the entire OT. It is a word composed of the first letters of → Torah, → Nebiim, and → Ketubim, the three major divisions of the Hebrew Bible.

**TANHUMA.** The rabbinic → midrash attributed to Rabbi Tanhuma bar Abba, latter fourth century A.D.; also known as → *Yelammedenu*.

**TANNAIM/TANNAITIC.** Collective name given to the earlier generations of rabbis (ca. first two centuries A.D.) who were duly qualified to expound the Scriptures with authority; some 120 scholars dating from the last of the → *zugoth*, Hillel and Shammai, to Judah Ha-Nasi, the compiler of the → Mishnah. The word *tanna*, "teacher," or "transmitter," was later applied to students who successfully learned the traditions. → Amoraim.

**TARGET LANGUAGE.** → Receptor Language.

**TARGUM.** A word that means literally "translation." Usually refers to translations of parts of the OT into → Aramaic, originating in the public reading of the OT in the synagogue, that involve a certain amount of interpretative comment or → paraphrase. *Ex:* the Targum of Onkelos (the Pentateuch) and the Targum of Jonathan (the Prophets).

**TARYAG.** A Hebrew word whose consonants form the numerical equivalent of 613, which is the number of laws that are said to be in the → Torah.

**TATIAN.** → Diatessaron.

**TAUTOLOGY.** The needless repetition of an idea in different words; a statement true by virtue of its logical form alone. *Ex:* widow *woman;* it rained *rain;* God *is divine.* → Redundancy, → Pleonasm.

**TECHNICAL TERM.** → Terminus Technicus.

**TEFILLIN.** → Tephillin.

**TEHILLIM.** Hebrew name ("praises") for the Book of Psalms.

**TELIC.** Words, → phrases, or → clauses that express purpose, tending toward an end or a conclusion; also called *final* or *purpose. Heb:* telic conjunctions are *lᵉmaʿan,* "in order that"; *pen,* "lest." *Gk:* telic conjunctions are *hopōs* and *hina,* "in order that," "so that."

**TEMPORAL.** The expression of duration or point in time. There are a number of ways of expressing the temporal idea in Hebrew and Greek. In Hebrew the preposition *beth* can mean "while." *Heb:* "And *while* they were in the field" (Gen. 4:8). Greek primarily utilizes particles in case constructions or verbal phrases to express time. *Gk:* "*When* his family *heard* about this, they went" (Mark 3:21).

**TEMPORAL AUGMENT.** → Augment.

**TEMPORAL CLAUSE.** A type of → adverbial clause that answers the question "when?"; it may indicate a time prior to, contemporary with, or subsequent to the verb action of the → main clause. *Heb:* "*While* his father Terah was still alive, Haran died" (Gen. 11:28). *Gk:* "*When* he had finished speaking, he said to Simon" (Luke 5:4).

**TENDENZ CRITICISM, TENDENCY CRITICISM.** The analysis and dating of the theological tendency of a biblical book, especially the bias with which a NT author interpreted his subject matter. The method is associated with F. C. Baur and the → Tübingen School, who saw the development of NT literature in terms of Petrine-Pauline conflict; thus, for example, Luke's tendency in Acts was to resolve the differences between Peter and Paul.

**TENSE.** In English grammar, the time of action indicated by a verb. In Greek, the time element appears only in the indicative → mood; the essential idea of Greek tense is kind of action (→ aspect). Hebrew is believed not to express tense, only completed and incompleted action, though some linguists disagree. Altogether, there are six tenses in English—present, past, future, present perfect, past perfect, and future perfect—that are paralleled in the translation of Hebrew and Greek verbs.

**TENSE STEM.** Addition of inflectional → affixes to the Greek verb → stem to indicate → tense. The six tense stems that remain intact throughout all the → conjugations are present, future, aorist, perfect, perfect middle, and aorist passive. → Principal Parts.

**TEN WORDS.** Another name for the → Decalogue.

**TEPHILLIN (sing. TEPHILLAH).** A phylactery or container worn by Jews that has copies of Deut. 6:4−9; 11:13−21; and Exod. 13:1−10, 11−16. The custom developed from an interpretation given to the → Shema.

**TERMINUS AD QUEM.** Latin for "limit to which." The end point of a chronological era or the latest date for an event.

**TERMINUS A QUO.** Latin for "limit from which." The starting point in time of a chronological era or the earliest date for an event.

**TERMINUS TECHNICUS.** Latin for a "technical term." Used of a word or phrase in a restricted sense within a field of study. Ex: → paradosis, → apothegm.

**TESTIMONIUM (pl., TESTIMONIA).** Latin for "evidence." An → explicit quotation of the OT adduced as a proof-text for the messiahship of Jesus, often with little explanation, and likely drawn from Christian → midrash-like anthologies.

**TETRAGRAM, TETRAGRAMMATON.** The name given to the Hebrew word for God, → Yahweh. It is composed of four letters in the Hebrew language (YHWH) and is usually translated as "the Lord," though sometimes as → Jehovah.

**TETRATEUCH.** A name given to the first four books of the OT.

**TEV.** An abbreviation for *Today's English Version* (also known as *Good News for Modern Man*); it is a very free translation into contemporary English, published in its entirety in 1976.

**TEXT.** The written or printed words in a → manuscript or book. The passage of Scripture selected for study, translation, or reading → Pericope

**TEXT-TYPE.** A major grouping of biblical → manuscripts, based on textual affinities, geographical proximity, and local → recensions. The three primary text-types are → *Alexandrian*, → *Western*, and → *Byzantine* or → *Lucianic*. → Family.

**TEXTUAL CRITICISM.** The discipline that attempts to reconstruct the original text of the Bible as nearly as can be determined. The procedure involves reconstruction of the history of transmission and assessment of the relative value of → manuscripts. The discipline is also called *lower criticism.*

**TEXTUAL EVIDENCE.** The cumulative evidence of various manuscripts for a particular → reading of the text.

**TEXTUS RECEPTUS.** The phrase means "received text." The text underlying the earliest printed editions of the Greek NT upon which the King James Version was based; a → Byzantine text-type published in two main editions by Stephanus (1550) and Elzevir (1633). Also used to designate any standard text, such as the → Ben Asher text of the OT.

**THAUMATURGY.** Another word for → magic; the performance of miracles or wonders.

**THEIOS ANER.** Greek for "divine man." A religious term in Greco-Roman paganism, applied to charismatic figures of superior wisdom, specially favored by the gods or in communion with them. → Aretalogy.

**THEMATIC VERB.** The class of Greek verbs that are inflected by the use of the → thematic vowel before the → personal endings. The other inflectional class, athematic or *mi* verbs, adds the endings directly to the tense stem. *Gk:* thematic: *erch* + *o* + *mai;* athematic: *tithē* + *mi.*

**THEMATIC VOWEL.** The vowel that characteristically appears with the second root letter of a Hebrew word; helpful in the identification of certain verbal → stems. In Greek, the final vowel of certain → tense stems that varies between *o* and *e* (lengthened to *ō* and *ē* in the → subjunctive mood). Also called *variable vowel.*

**THEOCRACY.** Government by the immediate direction of

God or through those who are His representatives. *Ex:* During the period of the Judges, Israel was a theocracy.

**THEODICY.** A vindication of the justice of God in permitting evil to exist. *Ex:* the Book of Job is a theodicy.

**THEODOTION.** Traditional name of a Greek version of the OT that represents a more literal rendering than the → LXX; it has affinities with the → Kaige recension. Little is known of Theodotion himself, who probably lived in the last half of the second century A.D. → Hexapla.

**THEOGONY.** The story of the birth and succession of the gods; an account of their generations or genealogy.

**THEOLOGOUMENON.** As a technical term, the content of theology proper, i.e., statements about God; by extension, a statement that is merely theological, demanded by neither divine revelation nor historical facts. *Ex:* "Sin is transmitted by heredity" is a theologoumenon.

**THEOMACHY.** Strife or warfare among the gods in pagan mythology. Also, a striving against God. *Ex:* Jacob, who wrestled all night with God (Gen. 32:24–32).

**THEOMORPHISM.** The belief that man has the form and likeness of God, based on Gen. 1:26–27. → Anthropomorphism.

**THEONOMY.** Rule by God; ethical teaching that moral law finds its ultimate authority in God Himself.

**THEOPATHY.** Religious ecstasy or mystical experience. *Ex:* the frantic dancing of the prophets of Baal (1 Kings 18:26–29).

**THEOPHANY.** A manifestation of God in a visible form. *Ex:* the burning bush (Exod. 3:1–5); the living creatures and throne (Ezek. 1:4–28). → Epiphany.

**THEOPHORIC, THEOPHOROUS.** A word that is derived from

or bearing the name of a god. *Ex:* Israel (→ El) means "he struggles with God" (Gen. 32:28).

**THEOPNEUST.** That which is divinely inspired.

**THERIOLATRY.** The worship of animals, common in biblical times, but consistently condemned in the Jewish and Christian faiths. *Ex:* Ezek. 8:9–11; Rom. 1:23.

**TIQQUNE SOPHERIM.** Corrections of the → scribes; the purpose was to remove objectional statements about God. There are eighteen of these in the → Masoretic text, e.g., Gen. 18:22; Num. 11:15. See Ernest Würthwein, *The Text of the Old Testament*, 2nd. ed., pp. 18–19, for a complete list.

**TMESIS.** Separation of parts of a compound word. *Ex:* "to what person soever" instead of "to whatsoever person."

**TONE-LONG VOWEL.** In Hebrew, a short vowel may become a long vowel under the influence of the accented (→ tone) syllable. Also called → *heightening. Ex: lā-mā-yim* for *lā-ma-yim* (Gen. 1:6).

**TONE SYLLABLE, TONIC SYLLABLE.** The syllable that receives the principal accent of the word in pronunciation.

**TORAH.** The word properly means "instruction." The name of the first division of the Hebrew Bible composed of the first five books; it is also called the → *Law.* → Nebiim, → Ketubim.

**TOSEPHTA.** A collection of → tannaitic traditions made from the third to the fifth centuries A.D.; arranged into six main divisions similar to the → Mishnah, but more → haggadic in nature and four times longer.

**TOUR DE FORCE.** French for "turn of force." A literary description of a work that provides an outstanding illustration of an author's skill; in critical reviews, often a work that has little merit except technical ingenuity.

**TRACTATE.** A treatise or essay; a book or section of the → Mishnah or → Talmud, e.g., the tractate → *Pirqe Aboth.*

**TRADENT.** Latin term for person or community that transmits the tradition. → Traditio.

**TRADITIO.** Latin, "tradition." The process of transmission as distinct from that which is transmitted (→ traditum).

**TRADITIO-HISTORICAL CRITICISM.** Another name for → tradition criticism.

**TRADITION CRITICISM, TRADITION HISTORY.** A study of the history of a tradition from its oral to its written stage. It is based on the belief that the material in the OT (and the NT to a lesser extent) passed through many generations by word of mouth before taking a fixed written form. This discipline is also called *traditio-historical criticism* and *oral tradition.* → Überlieferungsgeschichte.

**TRADITIONSGESCHICHTE.** A synonym for → Überlieferungsgeschichte.

**TRADITUM.** Latin for that which is transmitted. → Paradosis, → Traditio.

**TRANSCRIBE/TRANSCRIPTION.** To make an exact copy of a text, document, etc. Also, another term for → transliterate/ transliteration.

**TRANSITIVE.** A transitive verb has a receiver of the action to complete its meaning; it can have a passive → voice. *Heb:* "In the beginning God *created* the heavens and the earth" (Gen. 1:1). *Gk:* "He *gave* the right to become children of God" (John 1:12).

**TRANSLATION.** Transferring thoughts or writings from one language to another, while preserving the original meaning and intent of the author or speaker. Translation has also been used to describe the phenomenon of Enoch's (Gen. 5:24) and Elijah's (2 Kings 2:11) departing to be with God without experiencing death. → Dynamic Equivalence, → Formal Equivalence.

**TRANSLITERATE/TRANSLITERATION.** The writing of a Hebrew or Greek word with the equivalent letters of the English alphabet. It is also called transcription.

**TRANSPOSE/TRANSPOSITION.** To reverse or rearrange the usual order of letters or words.

**TRICOLA, TRICOLON.** Three colons (→ colon).

**TRILITERAL.** The three consonants that form the → root of most words in the Hebrew language.

**TRIPLE TRADITION.** The material that is common to all three → Synoptic Gospels, approximately 360 verses.

**TRISAGION.** Greek name for the "Holy, Holy, Holy" of Isa. 6:3.

**TRISTICH.** A larger grouping of lines of poetry composed of three lines. → Stich, Stichos.

**TRITO-ISAIAH.** Name given to the unknown author of Isaiah 56–66 by those who do not accept the unity of Isaiah. → Deutero-Isaiah.

**TRITO-ZECHARIAH.** The name given to the unknown author of Zechariah 12–14 by those who do not accept the unity of Zechariah. → Deutero-Zechariah.

**TROPE.** The use of a word in a sense other than its usual meaning; the figurative use of a word. Four types of trope are → *irony*, → *metaphor*, → *metonymy*, and → *synecdoche*.

**TROPOLOGY.** A method of biblical interpretation that seeks to discover the moral sense behind the literal meaning of a passage of Scripture.

**TÜBINGEN SCHOOL.** A school of NT interpretation centered in Tübingen, Germany, which flourished in the 1840s under its leader, F. C. Baur. Its chief endeavor was the application of the Hegelian dialectic to the development of primitive Christianity. → Tendenz Criticism.

**TUGENDKATALOG.** German term for a "catalog of virtues." → Ethical Lists, → Lasterkatalog.

**TWELVE, THE.** A designation of Jesus' twelve disciples (e.g., Matt. 26:14; Luke 8:1; John 6:67).

**TWO DOCUMENT HYPOTHESIS.** → Two Source Hypothesis.

**TWO GOSPEL HYPOTHESIS.** A name sometimes used for the → Griesbach hypothesis.

**TWO SOURCE HYPOTHESIS.** The most widely-accepted solution to the → Synoptic problem, developed in late nineteenth-century German scholarship. It postulates the priority of Mark; this earliest Gospel served as a major source for Matthew and Luke, and the latter two also used another common source, the sayings source, usually called → Q. The → hypothesis of Mark and Q (held in modified forms) now lacks critical consensus; also called the *two document hypothesis.* → Four Document Hypothesis, → Griesbach Hypothesis.

**TYPE/TYPOLOGY.** A method of biblical interpretation that sees persons, things, or events in the OT as foreshadowings or patterns ("types") of persons, things, or events in the NT, particularly as they occur within the framework of history as opposed to → allegory. *Ex:* Joseph as a type of Christ.

# U

**ÜBERLIEFERUNGSGESCHICHTE.** Also *Traditionsgeschichte;* German names for tradition history (→ tradition criticism); sometimes it is called the *traditiohistorical method.* It deals with the phase of oral tradition prior to the written composition.

**UBS³.** Abbreviation for → United Bible Societies' text of the Greek NT, third edition.

**UGARITIC.** An ancient Semitic language, similar to Hebrew and Phoenician; the language spoken by the inhabitants of Ugarit. This language is important for biblical studies because of the → Ras Shamra documents that are written in Ugaritic.

**ULTIMA.** In Greek, the last syllable of a word; when accented it is called the → *milraʿ* in Hebrew. → Oxytone, → Perispomenon.

**UNCIAL.** A kind of writing in which each letter was printed separately as a capital letter; also called –→ majuscule. The most important early Greek manuscripts of the Bible, more than 250 extant, written on → vellum or → parchment from the third to the eighth centuries A.D., are uncials. → Minuscule.

**UNITED BIBLE SOCIETIES' TEXT.** A → critical text of the Greek NT, now in its third edition (1975; referred to as

UBS[3]). It now prints the same text as the 26th edition of → Nestle-Aland; although its critical apparatus is more selective, the evidence cited is exhaustive for any → variant listed.

**UNKNOWN SAYINGS.** → Agrapha.

**UNPOINTED TEXT.** The Hebrew text written only with consonants; the vowels were omitted in early Hebrew writing and were added by the → Masoretes. → Pointing.

**UREVANGELIUM.** German for "primitive" or "original Gospel." The name assigned by G. E. Lessing to the lost → Aramaic document that was the common source of the → Synoptic Gospels. Also called *Urgospel, primitive Gospel,* or *original Gospel.*

**URGOSPEL.** Another name for → Urevangelium.

**URMARKUS.** German for "primitive" or "original Mark." The name assigned by H. J. Holtzmann to the hypothetical first stage of → canonical Mark, the assumption being that this → redaction was used by Matthew and Luke.

**URROLLE.** German for "original roll." A term used to indicate the earliest form of a biblical document, before any additions or → redactions were made. No Urrolle has been found to date. → Autograph.

**URTEXT.** A hypothetical primitive form of a biblical text that is no longer in existence.

**VARIABLE VOWEL.** Another name for → thematic vowel.

**VARIA LECTIO.** Latin term for → variant reading.

**VARIANT.** A different form or spelling of the same word. *Heb:* Jehoram (1 Kings 22:50), Joram (2 Kings 8:21). *Gk:* Priscilla (Acts 18:2), Prisca (Rom. 16:3).

**VARIANT READING.** A term used in → textual criticism to refer to differences in the wording of a biblical passage that are discovered by comparing different → manuscripts of the passage. *Ex:* a comparison of the → Masoretic text with the → LXX reveals a number of variants between the two texts. The → Dead Sea Scrolls have also revealed variants between the Masoretic text and these scrolls.

**VATICINIUM EX EVENTU.** A Latin term that means "prophecy or prediction made after the event." A disputed principle of → historical criticism that assumes that an event known to a biblical writer is turned into a prophecy by literary artifice. *Ex:* The Roman siege of Jerusalem known to Luke is placed back on the lips of Jesus as a prophecy (Luke 19:42–44; 21:20).

**VELARS.** Another name for → gutturals.

**VELLUM.** A leather writing material made from calfskin;

sometimes refers to a finer, more expensive product, but often synonymous with → parchment.

**VERB.** A part of speech that expresses action (such as *run, walk, see*) or state of being (such as *be, become*).

**VERBAL.** In traditional grammar, another name for the non-finite verbs (→ finite verb), the → participle, and the → infinitive; sometimes called *verbal adjective* and *verbal noun*.

**VERBAL ADJECTIVE.** Another name for → verbal.

**VERBAL INSPIRATION.** The belief that every word in the Bible is inspired by God. A corollary of this view is → inerrancy. Verbal inspiration should be distinguished from the → dictation theory in that the former is generally held to involve both divine and human authorship (→ paradox); frequently used as synonymous with → plenary inspiration.

**VERBAL NOUN.** Another name for → verbal.

**VERBAL SENTENCE.** In biblical languages, a sentence is verbal when its predicate contains a → finite verb; cf. → nominal sentence.

**VERB OF BEING.** Another name for → copula.

**VERB PHRASE.** In → generative grammars, another name for the → predicate.

**VERNACULAR.** The language of ordinary daily speech in a certain locality or region, as opposed to literary language. It frequently does not follow strict grammatical rules of correct usage.

**VERNACULAR KOINE.** → Koine Greek.

**VERSION.** A translation of the Bible from one language to another; frequently it is dependent on preceding translations. *Ex: King James Version, Revised Standard Version, New International Version.*

**VERSO.** The back of a → papyrus, where the strips run vertically as opposed to → recto; the outside of a → scroll. Sometimes writing was done on both sides of a scroll (→ opistograph). The left-hand page in a → codex and in our books.

**VETITIVE.** The normal way of expressing the imperative in Hebrew by the use of a negative → particle plus the → imperfect. *Heb:* "You shall not murder" (Exod. 20:13).

**VETUS LATINA.** Latin for → Old Latin.

**VID.** Abbreviation of Latin *videtur,* "apparently." Used in a → critical apparatus to indicate apparent support of a reading in a → manuscript whose state of preservation makes complete verification impossible.

**V.L.** Abbreviation of Latin *varia lectio,* "variant reading." Used in → textual criticism.

**VOCALIC.** Having the characteristics of or functioning as a vowel. → Sonants.

**VOCALIC AFFORMATIVE.** In Hebrew, an → afformative that begins with a vowel; it usually draws the accent to it. *Heb:* -āh, -û.

**VOCALIZATION.** Vocalization describes the addition of vowels to the Hebrew consonants; it is the same as → pointing.

**VOCATIVE.** The → case of address, denoting the person (or object) addressed. *Heb:* "Help us, *O God our Savior*" (Ps. 79:9). *Gk:* "*Master, Master,* we're going to drown!" (Luke 8:24). → Direct Address.

**VOICE.** Voice is a modification of a verb that tells whether the subject of the verb acts or is acted upon. There are three voices in English, Hebrew, and Greek: → active, → passive, and → reflexive.

**VOICED SOUND.** A voiced sound is one produced when the vocal cords vibrate as a result of the outgoing breath, thus producing the musical sound called the voice. Voiceless sounds are produced with the vocal cords slack. *Heb:* the ʿayin is described as a voiced ḥeth. *Gk:* compare voiced *beta* and voiceless *pi.*

**VOICELESS SOUND.** → Voiced Sound.

**VOLATILIZATION.** In Hebrew, when a short vowel or a tone-long vowel becomes a → half-vowel (simple or compound → *shewa*) the change is called volatilization.

**VOLITIVE.** Modal aspect of the verb expressing will, command, or request; it can appear in any of the three → persons. Also called *voluntative.* Comparable in force to the → jussive or → cohortative in Hebrew. In Greek, a regular use of the → subjunctive mood in prohibitions. *Heb:* "And God said, '*Let there be* light'" (Gen. 1:3). *Gk:* "*Let no one take* me for a fool" (2 Cor. 11:16).

**VOLUNTATIVE.** Another name for → volitive.

**VORLAGE.** German, "prototype." The underlying tradition behind a manuscript; a copy or → recension of a work used as a source.

**VOWEL.** A speech sound made by not blocking the oral part of the breath passage. In Hebrew syllables a vowel always follows a consonant, never precedes it (except for a furtive *pathaḥ*). For the names and pronunciation of the Hebrew and Greek vowels, see *Gesenius' Hebrew Grammar* (Kautzsch-Cowley 2nd ed.), sections 7–9; and Robertson's *New Short Grammar of the Greek Testament,* sections 28–33, 41.

**VOWEL CONTRACTION.** In Greek, the blending of adjacent vowels or → diphthongs into a long vowel or diphthong.

The structure of Hebrew does not allow contraction, but short vowels do combine with the → semivowels, *waw* and *yod*, to form diphthongs.

**VOWEL GRADATION.** A general process of → inflection by means of the alteration of internal vowels in a → stem, e.g., *sink, sank, sunk.* The graded change can be either quantitative (lengthening or shortening) or qualitative (changed in nature). *Heb:* short *a* becomes *i* (a qualitative change) in closed, unaccented syllables: *yaqṭul, yiqṭōl. Gk:* the tense stems of *leipō,* "I leave," show qualitative change: *leip-* (present), *-lip-* (aorist), and *-loip-* (perfect). → Attenuation.

**VOWEL LETTER.** → Matres Lectionis.

**VOWEL POINTS.** → Pointing.

**VULGATE.** A translation of the Bible into Latin by Jerome at the end of the fourth century A.D.; the "common" version of the medieval Catholic church. Jerome translated the OT directly from the Hebrew text current in his day; the NT is based on the → Old Latin and underwent curious revision.

**WAW CONJUNCTIVE.** In Hebrew a simple connective conjunction, usually translated as "and," but may also be translated as "but," "yet," "when," "so," "for," "since," "that," "how," "therefore," "then." It is also called the *light waw*, the *simple waw*, and the *copulative waw*.

**WAW CONSECUTIVE.** In Hebrew, a *waw* that may be prefixed to the → perfect and → imperfect forms of verbs; it will affect the meaning of the verb. Earlier grammars called it the *waw conversive*; it is also referred to as the *strong waw*. (See a Hebrew grammar for a full discussion of the *waw* consecutive.)

**WEAK VERB.** In Hebrew, the verbs with → gutturals or weak letters (*nun* in first root position, *yod* and *waw* in first or second root position, identical second and third root letters) as → radicals, which produce modifications in the → conjugation, in contrast to the → strong verb. In Greek, a → tense stem formed by adding a → suffix to the verb → stem or → root.

**WESTERN TEXT.** The NT → text-type associated with Rome and the Latin West. An unrevised text given to → paraphrase and → interpolation; its chief witness is → Codex Bezae. Also called *Delta text*.

WISDOM

**WISDOM.** Wisdom was a phenomenon of ancient Near Eastern culture that observed human experience and benefitted from it in order to gain mastery of life. It has been described as a quality of mind that distinguished the wise man from others (he is often contrasted with the "fool" in the OT). His wisdom enabled him to use factual knowledge to make proper judgments involving everyday living and so he was able to live well and enjoy success. Wisdom was also considered to be a quality inherent in God. Wise living in Israel was associated with following the precepts and counsel of God. Wise men exercised significant influence in the royal courts as well as among the common people. → Wisdom Literature.

**WISDOM LITERATURE.** The name given to a type of literature common to the ancient Near East. Job, Proverbs, and Ecclesiastes are the wisdom books of the OT, but wisdom writing is also found elsewhere in the OT. → Wisdom.

**WORD FORMATION.** The process of arranging → morphemes in the → composition of words to generate new forms. The two ways words are formed are → inflection (forms that signal grammatical relationships) and → derivation (forms that signal → lexical relationships).

**WORD ORDER.** In Hebrew, when a → finite verb is used in a → clause or emphasis is placed on the → predicate, the verb comes first; this pattern has heavily influenced the word order of the Greek NT. In both the OT and NT generally, priority of position is given to emphasized words. → Parataxis, → Periodic Sentence.

**WORDPLAY.** A play on words; also called → paronomasia.

**WRITINGS, THE.** The third division of the Hebrew Bible; also called the → *Hagiographa* or → *Ketubim.* → Torah, → Nebiim.

**YAHWEH, JAHWEH.** The name for God found most frequently in the OT; it occurs approximately 6823 times. It is the suggested pronunciation of the Hebrew → tetragram. The word is usually translated as "The Lord" but sometimes as "Jehovah" (based on a misunderstanding of the combination of the consonants of YHWH and the vowels of *Adonai*). Most English versions use "Lᴏʀᴅ" for Yahweh, "Lord" for Adonai; cf. Exod. 4:10.

**YAHWIST, JAHWIST.** In → literary criticism of the OT, the name given to the person believed to be the author of the oldest stratum of material in the → Pentateuch. This material is also called *J.* → JEDP.

**YELAMMEDENU.** A Hebrew word from the characteristic opening phrase of → homilies in the Midrash Tanhuma: *yelammedenu rabbenu,* "Let our master teach us." Each discourse is centered around an opening OT verse (→ proem text), poses a → halakic question, and proceeds with → haggadic → exposition.

# Z

**ZERO MORPHEME.** An abstract → morpheme, postulated by grammatical analysis but not written in Hebrew or Greek. Often the apparent absence of a suffix from a set of endings in a declension or conjugation; indicated by a #. *Heb:* The *qal* perfect, third person, masculine gender, singular form is zero morpheme as there is no suffix in this form. *Gk:* The aorist, active, indicative, third person, singular suffix is zero morpheme.

**ZEUGMA.** The use of a word to modify two or more words, with only one of which, however, it is appropriate, e.g., a verb that joins two objects while it actually is related to only one of them. *Heb:* "Take to yourself an adulterous wife and children" (Hos. 1:2); cf. Gen. 4:20. *Gk:* "I gave you [lit., gave you to drink] milk, not solid food" (1 Cor. 3:2); cf. Luke 1:64; 1 Tim. 4:3. → Syllepsis.

**ZUGOTH.** Hebrew, "pairs." A term applied to five generations of Jewish scholars preceding the → Tannaim, ca. first and second centuries B.C. The last pair were Hillel and Shammai. → Amoraim.

# Further Reference

The following works of reference will provide extended discussion of the entries in the glossary. The student should have at his fingertips *Webster's New Collegiate Dictionary* (Springfield, Mass.: G. & C. Merriam, 1977).

## Dictionaries and Encyclopedias

*Encyclopedia Judaica.* Edited by Cecil Roth. 16 vols. Jerusalem: Keter, 1971.

*The Interpreter's Dictionary of the Bible.* Supplementary volume. Edited by Keith Crim. Nashville: Abingdon, 1976.

*The New International Dictionary of the Christian Church.* Rev. ed. Edited by J. D. Douglas and Earle E. Cairns. Grand Rapids: Zondervan, 1978.

*The New International Dictionary of New Testament Theology.* Edited by Colin Brown. 3 vols. Grand Rapids: Zondervan, 1976–1978.

*The New Standard Jewish Encyclopedia.* Rev. ed. Edited by Cecil Roth and Geoffrey Wigoder. Jerusalem: Massada, 1970.

*The Oxford Classical Dictionary.* 2nd ed. Edited by N. G. L. Hammond and H. H. Scullard. New York: Oxford University Press, 1970.

## Commentaries

*The Expositor's Bible Commentary.* Vol. 1: *Introductory Articles.* Edited by Frank E. Gaebelein. Grand Rapids: Zondervan, 1979.

*The Jerome Bible Commentary.* Edited by Raymond E. Brown,

Joseph A. Fitzmyer, and Roland E. Murphy. Englewood Cliffs, N.J.: Prentice-Hall, 1968.

### Hebrew and Greek Texts

*Biblia Hebraica.* 3rd ed. Edited by Rudolf Kittel and Paul Kahle. Stuttgart: Württembergische Bibelanstalt, 1937.

*Biblia Hebraica Stuttgartensia.* Edited by K. Elliger and W. Rudolph. Stuttgart: Deutsche Bibelstiftung, 1977.

*The Greek New Testament.* 3rd ed. Edited by K. Aland et al. New York: United Bible Societies, 1975.

*Novum Testamentum Graece.* 26th ed. Edited by Kurt Aland and Dieter Nestle. Stuttgart: Deutsche Bibelgesellschaft, 1979.

### Lexicons and Concordances

Arndt, W. F.; Gingrich, F. W.; and Danker, F. W. *A Greek-English Lexicon of the New Testament.* 2nd ed. Chicago: University of Chicago Press, 1979.

Brown, Francis; Driver, S. R.; and Briggs, C. A. *A Hebrew and English Lexicon of the Old Testament.* Oxford: Clarendon Press, 1952.

Holladay, William L., ed. *A Concise Hebrew and Aramaic Lexicon of the Old Testament.* Grand Rapids: Eerdmans, 1971.

Lisowsky, Gerhard. *Konkordanz zum hebräischen Alten Testament.* Stuttgart: Württembergische Bibelanstalt, 1958.

Moulton, W. F., and Geden, A. S. *A Concordance to the Greek Testament.* 5th ed. Revised by H. K. Moulton. Edinburgh: T. & T. Clark, 1978.

### Grammars

Blass, F., and Debrunner, A. *A Greek Grammar of the New Testament.* Translated and revised by Robert W. Funk. Chicago: University of Chicago Press, 1961.

Davidson, A. B. *Hebrew Syntax.* 3rd ed. Edinburgh: T. & T. Clark, 1901.

Gesenius, W., and Kautzsch, E. *Gesenius' Hebrew Grammar.* 2nd ed. Revised by A. E. Cowley. Oxford: Clarendon Press, 1910.

Lambdin, Thomas O. *An Introduction to Biblical Hebrew.* New York: Scribner's, 1971.

LaSor, William S. *Handbook of Biblical Hebrew.* Vol. 2. Grand Rapids: Eerdmans, 1979.

_____. *Handbook of New Testament Greek.* Vol. 2. Grand Rapids: Eerdmans, 1973.

Moulton, J. H.; Howard, W. F.; and Turner, Nigel. *A Grammar of New Testament Greek.* 4 vols. Edinburgh: T. & T. Clark, 1908–1976.

Robertson, A. T. *A Grammar of the Greek New Testament in the Light of Historical Research.* Nashville: Broadman, 1947.

Robertson, A. T., and Davis, W. H. *A New Short Grammar of the Greek New Testament.* 10th ed. New York: Harper & Brothers, 1933.

Vaughan, Curtis, and Gideon, Virtus E. *A Greek Grammar of the New Testament.* Nashville: Broadman, 1979.

Weingreen, J. *A Practical Grammar for Classical Hebrew.* 2nd ed. Oxford: Clarendon Press, 1959.

### Linguistics

Crystal, David. *A First Dictionary of Linguistics and Phonetics.* London: Andre Deutsch, 1980.

Gleason, Henry A. *An Introduction to Descriptive Linguistics.* 2nd ed. New York: Rinehart and Winston, 1961.

Nida, Eugene A., and Taber, Charles R. *The Theory and Practice of Translation.* Helps for Translators, vol. 8. Leiden: United Bible Societies, 1969.

### English Grammar

Pence, R. W., and Emery, D. W. *A Grammar of Present-Day English,* 2nd ed. New York: Macmillan, 1963.

Roberts, Paul. *Understanding Grammar.* New York: Harper & Row, 1954.

Seaton, Brian. *A Handbook of English Language Teaching Terms and Practice.* New York: Macmillan, 1982.

Zandvoort, R. W. *A Handbook of English Grammar.* 7th ed. London: Longman, 1975.

### Textual Criticism

Finegan, Jack. *Encountering New Testament Manuscripts.* Grand Rapids: Eerdmans, 1974.

Kenyon, F. G. *The Text of the Greek Bible.* 3rd ed. Revised by A. W. Adams. London: Duckworth, 1975.

Metzger, Bruce M. *The Text of the New Testament.* 2nd ed. New York: Oxford University Press, 1968:

————. *A Textual Commentary on the Greek New Testament.* New York: United Bible Societies, 1971.

Weingreen, J. *Introduction to the Critical Study of the Text of the Hebrew Bible.* New York: Oxford University Press, 1982.

Würthwein, Ernst. *The Text of the Old Testament.* Translated by E. F. Rhodes. Grand Rapids: Eerdmans, 1979.

## Literary Criticism

Bühlmann, Walter and Scherer, Karl. *Stilfiguren der Bibel. Ein kleines Nachschlagewerk.* Biblische Beiträge 10. Fribourg: Schweizerisches Katholisches Bibelwerk, 1973.

Caird, George B. *The Language and Imagery of the Bible.* Philadelphia: Westminster, 1980.

Cuddon, J. A. *A Dictionary of Literary Terms.* Rev. ed. New York: Doubleday, 1980.

Lanham, Richard A. *A Handlist of Rhetorical Terms: A Guide for Students of English Literature.* Berkeley: University of California, 1980.

Wellek, Rene, and Warren, Austin. *Theory of Literature.* Rev. ed. New York: Harcourt Brace, 1956.

## Historical Criticism

Anderson, G. W., ed. *Tradition and Interpretation.* New York: Oxford University Press, 1979.

Eissfeldt, Otto. *The Old Testament: An Introduction.* New York: Harper & Row, 1965.

Koch, Klaus. *The Growth of the Biblical Tradition.* Translated by S. M. Cupitt. New York: Scribner's, 1968.

Kümmel, W. G. *Introduction to the New Testament.* 17th rev. ed. Translated by H. C. Kee. Nashville: Abingdon, 1975.

Marshall, I. Howard, ed. *New Testament Interpretation.* Grand Rapids: Eerdmans, 1978.

Soulen, Richard N. *Handbook of Biblical Criticism.* 2nd ed. Atlanta: John Knox, 1981.

Turner, Nicolas. *Handbook for Biblical Studies.* Oxford: Basil Blackwell, 1982.